GARDENING IN YOUR APARTMENT

GARDENING IN YOUR APARTMENT

CREATING AN INTERIOR OASIS

Gilly Love
Special photography by Michelle Garrett

LORENZ BOOKS

For Malcolm Riddell, a very special gardener, who gave me my much treasured Sparmannia.

This edition first published in 1996 by Lorenz Books

© DuMont Buchverlag GmbH und Co. Kommandit gesellschaft
Koln, Federal Republic of Germany, 1995

Lorenz Books is an imprint of
Anness Publishing Limited
1 Boundary Row
London SE1 8HP

This edition distributed in Canada by
Raincoast Book Distribution Limited

ISBN 1 85967 104 7

A CIP catalogue record for this book is available from the British Library.

Publisher: Joanna Lorenz
Project Editor: Judith Simons
Designer: Lisa Tai
Special photography: Michelle Garrett
Illustrator: Anna Koska

Typeset by MC Typeset Limited
Printed and bound in Italy

Acknowledgements
With special thanks to: **Michelle Garrett** for her wonderful photographs, which have brought my words and ideas
to life, and her assistant, **Dulcie**, who kindly lent her hands for many of the practical pictures;
Chryssie Lowe who designed and created the delightful stencilled pots on pages 56 and 57;
Rosie Atkins, editor of *Gardens Illustrated*, for her immense generosity and infectious enthusiasm for plants and flowers;
Veronica Richardson of The Flowers & Plants Association for her advice and support;
Judith Simons, project editor, whose understanding, endless patience and encouragement helped me to create
this book; and **Lisa Tai** for her sensitive and creative layout of the book.

Thanks also to: **Stephen Woodhams** for allowing us to photograph his roof terrace and apartment;
Susie and **Roger Black**, and **John Freeman** and **Vanessa Ephson** for permission to photograph their apartments;
Joan Clifton of **Avant Garden** for loaning plant containers featured on pages 30, 51, 69, 81 and 119;
Peter Watkins of **MKM Nurseries** for supplying plants; **Sandersons** for supplying Quartet wallpaper
and fabric on page 38.

Contents

INTRODUCTION

Planning an interior garden is just like
decorating and furnishing your home – a balance
between aspiration, what is practically possible,
and the time you have to spare.
Careful assessment of the space and light
your apartment can provide will help you to
choose the plants best suited to it.

Living Colour

Flowers and plants can instantly change the whole atmosphere of your home, and with the ever-expanding range of flowering plants you can quickly vary a room's colour scheme and mood from season to season. Even in the tiniest of apartments there is space for a

bowl of fragrant spring bulbs, pots of basil for summer salads, a basket of autumnal chrysanthemums and a window box filled with brightly coloured cyclamen to cheer up dull winter months. Although long-term evergreen plants still remain popular, short-lived flowering varieties give instant pleasure and can be used to create stunning indoor displays of colour. However, when their flowering season is over, they should be discarded and replaced just as an arrangement of cut flowers would be.

Most houseplants originate from the tropical regions of the world and, although plant breeders have produced hybrid species that are better able to tolerate domestic interiors, you may never be able to re-create their natural habitat. Accurately assessing the environment you can provide should help you to choose plants that will cohabit most happily with you. An indoor bougainvillea is never going to resemble the glorious specimens that flourish in their natural tropical habitats, unless it is provided with a conservatory or a large sun-filled window for most of the year. And even the most green-fingered gardener will not be able to make a shade- and humidity-loving fern thrive in a sunny window. Most of the

OPPOSITE Most plants, with the exception of some shade-loving ferns, enjoy the light from a west-facing window. Grouping plants together at floor level enables the light to reach into the rest of the room.

OPPOSITE **Bambusa vulgaris** *(common bamboo) grows wild in most tropical regions of the world but it has only recently been cultivated as a houseplant. A modern-looking plant which suits contemporary interiors, it is ideal for conservatories or sunny windows.*

LEFT **Eustoma grandiflorum** *(prairie gentian) is one of the new generation of short-term houseplants intended to be discarded after flowering.*

popular varieties of plants have become so because they are easy to look after and can tolerate a wide range of conditions.

In this book you will find practical advice on choosing plants that will best suit you and your home, simple ideas for displaying and grouping plants and how to make the most of colour and scent. There is a section on creating different decorative effects for kitchens and bathrooms, bedrooms and living rooms, bearing in mind their differing conditions and varying functions. Some ideas are long-term but many, such as those in the chapter devoted to the four seasons, are designed to be quick, easy and temporary so that your apartment can be kept constantly refreshed with living colour.

Assessing Your Site

ABOVE Full-sun-loving plants include cacti, brightly coloured bougainvillea, Kalanchoe, Echeveria and other succulents, citrus trees, the exotic Nerium oleander (oleander) and most flowering plants such as the Osteospermum.

*U*nless your apartment receives no natural light whatsoever, it will be possible to raise the majority of houseplants successfully, providing, that is, you give them the other vital ingredients that they need: water, humidity and warmth. It is not reasonable, however, to expect that all houseplants will last forever – some will survive for only a few months in average conditions, others will go on for a couple of years before they become straggly and unattractive, and only the toughest plants will really flourish for any longer than that.

The golden rule which can be applied to finding a suitable location for most houseplants is consistent moderation: a position that provides good indirect light for most of the day will suit virtually any plant. If a likely position does not immediately present itself to you, try experimenting by changing the room around. For instance, a book case repositioned closer to a window will provide a shelf for greenery; while replacing curtains with blinds will open up a permanent spot for an internal window box if there is sufficient room on the sill.

Once you have given a plant a position, leave it there; constantly changing places is very disturbing to a plant and is often the cause of leaf drop because the plant will register a move as a change in season. Regular care will also make a

OPPOSITE A collection of floor-standing Musa makes two simple arrangements. The containers have been chosen to blend with the wooden floor.

BELOW Scented Pelargonium (geranium) need full sun, poor soil and moderate watering to produce flowers throughout the summer months.

FAR LEFT A small but high-ceilinged room demands tall, thin plants like this Ficus longifolia *and* Ficus benghalensis.

LEFT The constant overhead light from a skylight and the gentle humidity provided by a warm bathroom suit most palms and ferns, and it is the ideal location for this water-loving Cyperus.

substantial difference to a plant's longevity. Overwatering and wild fluctuations in temperature will kill most plants in a matter of weeks and, in some cases, days.

If you are considering getting a large, mature specimen, make sure that you have just the right place for it before you make an investment. Many garden centres and plant specialists offer an advice service and, for a small fee, and sometimes for free, a qualified professional will assess and recommend the best choice of plants for your home.

LIGHT

Natural light is the one element vital to plants that is determined by the size, proportion and, most crucially, aspect of your apartment's windows. Whatever the size of window, it is the direction in which it faces that has the most profound effect on the quality and intensity of light that it receives. An east-facing window gets the early morning sun, which is substantially cooler than the light at midday or during the afternoon. Providing there are no obstructions immediately in front of the window such as tall buildings or large, densely leaved trees, most plants will thrive here, including flowering plants that are in flower or have mature buds. West-facing windows generally receive a stronger, hotter light as a result of the sun's increased intensity towards the end of the day. With the exception of shade-loving plants such as ferns, and

Aglaonema, *Fittonia* and *Peperomia*, most plants enjoy this aspect. If a west-facing window has an external sill as well as an inside window shelf, this will be a good place for an outside window box in spring and summer; during autumn and winter, bring the box inside and fill it with a display of seasonal plants.

Sun-loving plants adore south-facing windows (north-facing windows in the Southern hemisphere) and many exotic flowering plants will thrive and grow in profusion here, including bougainvillea, *Nerium oleander* (oleander), *Pelargonium* (geranium), hibiscus, succulents, cacti and all the citrus varieties. As growth can be prolific, you may have to prune plants regularly to keep their shape.

The last aspect, the north facing window (south-facing in the Southern hemisphere), receives the least light and no sun. This can make north-facing rooms rather gloomy, but many tropical plants can tolerate poor light provided they are given sufficient warmth and humidity. Rooms such as these benefit enormously from an arrangement of deep green plants that add living colour.

Once the advantages and limitations of each aspect have been addressed, the proportion of each window can come into play when choosing suitable plants. The area in front of full-length windows is the obvious location for numerous varieties, but, if the windows also act as walkways between a balcony or patio, ease of access must be considered when siting the plants. In winter, however, when outside access is not so critical, use this additional floor space to store tropical plants that have been outdoors for the spring and summer months and need winter protection from frost.

Leave the area clear immediately in front of each window to allow the maximum light to penetrate the room for the benefit of those plants positioned further inside. Small windows, on the other hand, let in little light and, particularly if they have no view, are often improved by a screen of plants. You can create this effect either by placing the plants on glass shelves fitted across the window or by using plants that are tall enough to fill the entire frame.

Wide windows provide the opportunity to mix a whole variety of plant sizes and shapes while still allowing light to reach the rest of the room. If the floor space in front of a window is free of furniture, use this to make an impact with several specimen plants. As an alternative, position a low table beneath the window for a display of small plants that prefer indirect light: *Chlorophytum comosum* (spider plant), *Peperomia glabella*, *Fittonia*, *Tolmiea menziesii* (piggyback plant) and many of the ivies. All these trailing plants can also be made to climb; kept in close proximity to each other, the

impact of their varied foliage is intensified, not to mention the benefits of the increased humidity created in the atmosphere around the plants.

There are a few care considerations that need to be kept in mind when growing plants at windows. Plants placed directly in front of a window receive light from one direction only and must be turned regularly to ensure even growth. Unless you have double glazing, avoid the sandwich effect of plants caught between glass and curtains at night, particularly in winter, when this is often the coldest position in the room. During the

LEFT Pelargonium *(geranium),* Euphorbia milii, Zantedeschia aethiopica *and* Crassula argentea *need a brightly lit window to blossom.*

day, the light from a hot sunny window may be too strong for anything but the hardiest of desert cacti. A roller blind or Venetian blind will give you control of the light levels and keep less light-tolerant plants warm but shaded.

WATER AND HUMIDITY

Most apartments have some form of central heating and the dry atmosphere this creates can be as uncomfortable to humans as it is damaging to the majority of houseplants. In their natural habitat, most tropical plants grow under a canopy of leaves provided by the rainforest, and humidity is therefore constantly high all year round. Commercial plant growers have now developed hybrids that are better suited to conditions in the modern home, but it is still true that the higher the humidity, the better the plant's appearance. The majority of houseplants can survive in lower levels of humidity, particularly in summer when windows are open and there is a good circulation of air. In winter, when the heating is turned on, the humidity levels plummet and as a result leaf tips turn brown and curl up, young leaves fail to develop and flower buds drop off before opening.

Commercial room humidifiers will rectify the balance between heat and moisture, but they are an expensive option if one is needed in each room. A careful selection of plants that do not require very humid conditions is a more economical solution to the problem,

perhaps reserving a few of the more demanding varieties for a warm bathroom. Misting moisture-loving plants on a daily basis gives instant if not longlasting relief, and acts as a useful reminder to check delicate specimens regularly. Standing a plant on a tray of wet pebbles, keeping the water level below the base of the plant pot, will increase the humidity in the immediate vicinity of the plant. When several small plants are grouped together, surround the pots with wet pebbles and add a thick carpet of moss to the top of the soil to hold in moisture. These simple measures

will also improve the general atmosphere of the room and inhibit the drying effects of central heating and air conditioning.

When it comes to watering plants, make life easier by not positioning plants in difficult-to-reach places – they will only get forgotten and die. Allocate a regular time each week to water plants, and invest in a proper watering can with a long spout. If you have a patio or roof terrace, consider installing an outside tap. This will prove invaluable in the summer when the pots will dry out very quickly and will need a good dousing at least once a day.

Choosing the Right Plants

*BELOW RIGHT Many
plants may be
considered long-
lasting, including:
(back, left to right)
Syngonium, Hedera
canariensis,
Aglaonema; (front,
left to right) Pteris
ensiformis, Hedera
helix (common ivy),
and Chamaedorea
elegans.*

*G*ardening of any sort is immensely satisfying and only becomes a chore when the work outweighs the benefits. If you are starting an indoor garden from scratch, begin slowly, gradually building up a collection of plants as your confidence and expertise develop. To begin with, one truly magnificent specimen plant may be all a room needs, and, if you have chosen wisely, it should not need more care than you are willing or able to provide. But remember, the larger the plant, the greater the financial investment and, if it is to look its best, usually the more expensive the container.

As a general rule, most plants are simple to look after if they are given the right conditions, and they will reward you with an attractive and developing appearance that in some cases will result in flowers or colourful bracts. It is only when, for instance, certain plants need a moisture-laden atmosphere at all times that they fall into the high-maintenance category. Some plants require very exacting conditions which the average apartment is incapable of supplying. A *Phalaenopsis* (moth orchid), for example, must be kept at 25°C (77°F) in summer, stored in cool conditions in winter, and

OPPOSITE In a poorly lit room, daylight may be boosted with the help of fluorescent tubes. Here, grasses and bamboos are combined with dried reeds for contrasting colour and texture.

FAR RIGHT Orchids, lilies, miniature roses, Pelargonium (geranium), begonias and chrysanthemums are popular short-term flowering plants. Hypoestes sanguinolenta and Adiantum (maidenhair fern) can also be short-lived as they are quite difficult to maintain.

*LEFT Variegated foliage and contrasting leaf
shapes and sizes provide interest in a collection of
evergreen plants, with subtle colour provided by
the ceramic containers. Grouping plants together
also increases the humidity level.*

given at least ten hours of natural or artificial light every day if it is to flower the following year. At the other end of the spectrum, a *Monstera deliciosa* (Swiss cheese plant) will tolerate a moderate amount of light and normal room temperatures, and will not object to central heating. Although it will survive in these conditions, regular feeding in spring and summer, a high level of humidity and a little extra light in winter will see it rapidly grow and flourish.

When you are starting an indoor garden, how easy a plant is to care for will be your first consideration, but you should always try to vary your choice of plants to complement the style of your rooms. The bold shape and dark shiny leaves of a *Ficus lyrata* are too aggressive for the pastel and soft tones of a prettily

decorated bedroom, whereas the variegated heart-shaped leaves of a *Caladium bicolor* hybrid blend well with delicate colours. Placing the plant in a pale green or pink planter to pick up the colour of the leaves, and standing this on a tray of pale pink or creamy stones with more of the same stones covering the soil, would make the overall effect more attractive while providing essential humidity.

Consider too how plants will look at night. A couple of carefully placed spotlights or uplighters will illuminate the plants and create interesting dappled shadows on the walls and ceilings. The cheapest method is to use one or two clip spotlights clamped to the side of the pot or the tray beneath. Place them at the back of the plant so that the effect is not spoilt by the mechanics. Uplighters

are plastic or metal cylinders, usually about 20 cm (8 in) high, containing a single bulb which throws light directly upwards. They create an attractive mosaic of shadow patterns on the ceiling if they are positioned directly behind a large floor-standing plant with small- to medium-sized leaves.

Other practical considerations need to be taken into account when choosing and displaying plants. Floor space may well be the only place for plants but this is not an ideal position if there are inquisitive dogs, cats or small children in the apartment. Fragile leaves are easily damaged and an expanse of soft, bare earth may be too much of a temptation for even the best-trained pet. Cats that have little or no access to the outside world may consider a woody stem perfect for sharpening their claws, and they seem to like nothing better than to curl up on a fragile fern. Many houseplants are poisonous or can cause allergic reactions and should be avoided if there are young children in the apartment.

If the apartment is completely devoid of natural light, there is always the option of fake plants. There are some very realistic-looking false plants available made from silk or other fabrics, but do

ABOVE White-flowered Pelargonium (geranium) *provide a dense, bushy shape in an outdoor window box and complement the soft colour scheme of the room.*

avoid anything made from plastic. A couple of well-chosen varieties combined with a few short-lived flowering plants is far better than no plants at all.

EASY-CARE COLLECTIONS

Most indoor gardens consist of a combination of perennials and annuals or, more precisely, those plants that last for years and those that are seasonal. If you cannot bear to throw any plants away, then select perennials that will thrive in the conditions that you can provide easily. Long-lasting plants that are easy to care for include aspidistra, *Beaucarnea recurvata*, *Chlorophytum comosum* (spider plant) and most of the *Cissus*, *Dracaena*, *Fatsia* and *Ficus* families. Generally, climbing ivies such as *Hedera helix* (common ivy) and *Rhoicissus rhomboidea* (grape ivy) require little maintenance; *Schefflera*, tradescantia and very hardy yucca are also excellent plants for beginners.

Most of the members of the bromeliad family are interesting to collect, and are easy to maintain given constant warmth and good light. They all have quite spreading forms and need space around them to be appreciated. Ferns too have bushy and spreading shapes, but their soft leaves and branches mean that they can be grouped more closely together, which also improves humidity levels.

If your apartment can offer constant heat and plenty of sunlight, desert cacti and succulents are a good choice and will be very easy to look after.

DESIGNING YOUR INTERIOR GARDEN

Plants can create an interior style of their own or can be used to enhance existing decorations in your apartment. Flowering plants add a further dimension by either complementing or contrasting with interior colour schemes.

Displaying Plants

The architectural style of your apartment and the way it is decorated will affect the choice of plants you display there. Some plant forms are better matched to certain types of interiors than others. Traditional interiors tend to suit small plants that complement fabrics, wallpapers and other furnishings. Starkly decorated modern rooms can take a bolder statement in the form of larger, more sculptural plants. To be avoided at all costs is the single, sickly looking specimen in an ill-fitting container where the plastic inner pot sticks up over the planter, betraying both a lack of care and sensitivity to living things. The other main considerations to take into account when selecting plants for your home are the size of the plants in relation to the room area, the way that they grow – climbing, trailing, bushy or upright – and their shape and colour.

PLANTS AND SCALE

If plants are to make a positive addition to an interior, they must be compatible with the space in terms of both size and shape. A large specimen *Ficus*, *Dracaena*, *Chrysalidocarpus lutescens* (areca palm) or *Howea*, for example, needs a spacious, high-ceilinged room in order to spread its elegant, arching branches and to make a

OPPOSITE The arching branches of Phoenix canariensis *emphasize the simple lines of a modern interior. Raised from the floor, the plant is neatly framed within the window.*

RIGHT A formal symmetry is created with a pair of topiary Hedera helix *(common ivy); they need to be regularly pruned to maintain their precise shape and turned every week to ensure even growth.*

suitably dramatic impact. Try squeezing any one of these plants into a small area and it will simply overpower the room's proportions, and may make walking from one side of the room to the other more like cutting through a jungle. Unlike many garden plants and shrubs, these indoor varieties generally grow very slowly, and are cultivated in a wide range of heights. If the room requires a 2 m (6 ft) palm, select one at that height or

ABOVE During the summer months when the fireplace is not in use, a mantelshelf will provide a display area for plants, such as these pretty pots of Hedera helix *(common ivy).*

slightly smaller – you could wait a long time for a 1 m (3 ft) specimen to fill the space you have allowed for it.

If you want height and a compact shape, select a climbing plant that can be trained to grow up a mossed pole or

bamboo stake. Ivies will naturally wrap themselves around poles and stakes and with a little pruning can be trained into the desired shape very easily. *Hedera canariensis* is an attractive ivy with large leaves which come in all-green or variegated forms splashed with silver, grey or white markings. *Fatshedera lizei* (ivy tree) is a modern hybrid created by crossing *Fatsia japonica* with *Hedera helix* (common ivy). The resulting ivy tree grows to

ABOVE The lush, bushy shapes of Soleirolia soleirolii *make an ideal choice for a low coffee table. These plants can tolerate bright, indirect light or semi-shady conditions.*

around 2 m (6 ft), and several plants grown together in a large container soon make a tower of green or variegated foliage. Although *F. lizei* prefers a particularly good light, it can tolerate less well-lit areas, which makes it a good choice for the corner of a room.

TIERED DISPLAYS

Shelving is another useful way to gain height, with the added advantage that you can display a range of plants in one self-contained unit. A multi-tiered *étagère* is a specially designed piece of plant furniture, consisting of an upright from which stem six or seven small square or circular shelves. It is often made from wrought iron, and was particularly popular in Victorian garden rooms. Originals are much sought-after, but authentic reproductions are now avaialble thanks to the revived popularity of conservatories. The advantage of an *étagère* is that the whole stand is easily turned to ensure the regular growth of all the plants it supports. A combination of trailing and more bushy plants will fill the shelves to give a tall, green shape of similar tones.

ABOVE Scindapsus aureus *is an easy, fast-growing ivy that may be trained to grow around a window frame. Several pots of tradescantia trail profusely to add dense colour to a plain wall.*

RIGHT Fatshedera lizei *(ivy tree) is a modern hybrid, a cross between* Fatsia japonica *and* Hedera helix *(common ivy). It can be easily trained to make an attractive green frame around both doors and windows.*

As a variation, create a striped sandwich effect by interspersing green plants with the seasonal colours of *Campanula* (bell-flower) or chrysanthemum. A tall *étagère* is also the place to show off a collection of one species of plant such as *Begonia rex*, which has an enormous variety of hybrids with different leaf shapes, colours and markings.

The advantage of fixed shelving is that it can be used to combine both display areas for plants and storage for other items. Fitting triangular shelves in the corner of a room is an economical way of providing a permanent plant-display area. Floor-to-ceiling shelving using a material such as medium-density fibreboard may only require fixing with narrow battens if the shelves are supporting small, light-weight pot plants. Painted the colour of the walls or matched totally with the wallpaper, the shelves simply merge into the background, making the plants the focus of attention.

Higher shelves and those above shoulder level should be filled with cascading varieties to avoid only the container being seen, with lower shelves devoted to upward-growing types of plants. *Kalanchoe manginii* is ideal for upper shelves, as the flower-laden branches hang downwards, completely concealing the pot. Flowering plants such as fuchsia or *Pelargonium* (geranium) also suit these higher positions, and more permanent green plants include *Pellaea rotundifolia* (button fern) and *Asparagus falcatus*.

COLOUR

Colour is another important consideration when it comes to choosing plants for your home. A delicate paint effect or softly toned wallpaper can be swamped by heavy, dark green foliage. However, the pale fronds of fragile ferns or pastel and white flowering plants will enhance a gentle colour scheme rather than dominate it. Pale plain-coloured walls will complement most plants, but introducing foliage or flowering plants into a scheme with floral or patterned wallpaper and

furnishings needs more thought. Take a piece of the fabric or wallpaper with you to the garden centre or plant specialist and use this to help you select an appropriate shade of green.

With the huge selection of seasonal flowering plants available, it is quite feasible to create a continuity of colour with

BELOW Plants may be used to create a natural divider. In this kitchen-dining room, a wide trough of foliage plants obscures the functional part of the kitchen from the dining area.

different varieties throughout the year. For instance, furnishings that feature contrasting tones of blue and yellow may be matched with the living colours of *Eustoma* and primula in summer, or with hyacinth and narcissi in spring.

PRACTICAL DISPLAYS

As well as being decorative, plants can have practical applications too. A windowful of herbs not only provides a fresh source of flavourings for the pot, but also offers an alternative to curtains. With

ABOVE This wrought-iron candle sconce has been designed to incorporate a small plant such as this ivy. Be careful not to let the candle burn too low and scorch the leaves of the plant.

this in mind, consider widening a windowsill to provide a deeper platform for plants. A recessed window fitted with narrow glass or solid shelves provides the ideal support for a display of small bushy or trailing plants; while light-loving climbers will quickly provide a green curtain right to the top of the window if the plants are given a series of thin wires to clamber up. Climbers can also be encouraged to act as a frame. A climbing plant trained to scramble around a large picture hanging above a mantelpiece, for instance, looks stunning.

If siting plants at the window, it is essential to select ones that can tolerate hot summer rays or at the very least strong, bright light. In apartments with no outside access, this window space provides a temporary home for plants that need intense light, such as bougain-villea, *Pelargonium* (geranium), hibiscus or *Nerium oleander* (oleander). Once they are in flower, they can be transferred to a more eye-catching position before being moved on again to a resting space.

A light, bright room may be partially separated by using a group of tall plants

ABOVE This Phalaenopsis (moth orchid) provides a graceful organic touch to a collection of wall-mounted ceramics, perfectly complementing the simple shapes and colour scheme of the stone-coloured vases.

to create a room divider, usually partitioning, say, a dining space from a sitting area. As an alternative, fill an open shelving unit in the centre of a similarly well-lit room with plants that are viewed from both sides. If the light levels on te lower shelves prohibit living plants, use them for storing books or displaying other inanimate objects instead. Hanging baskets can also be used to furnish alcoves or act as room dividers, although they are not as fashionable as they once were. Suspended straw baskets and tasselled macrame pot holders are entirely appropriate in Mediterranean-, Spanish- or Mexican-style homes, but look out of place with fitted carpets and an upholstered three-piece suite. Contemporary designs of candelabra offer a better solution here, with pots hanging from the various arms. Some candelabra even come with a central area specifically designed to hold a potted plant.

GROUPING PLANTS

Metal wall sconces designed to hold candles are easily adapted for trailing plants. Decorative wire wall containers for bathroom and kitchen accessories also make excellent pot holders. A group of these arranged closely together creates a considerable impact. Table-top displays are the other obvious choice for many rooms, but most plants hate being moved around, so it is important that they can be left in peace. Narrow console tables require little space and are ideal for the purpose.

LEFT A permanent display of plants in glass containers on metal and glass shelving fills a small window and makes an attractive alternative to curtains or blinds.

If the space around the table is restricted, limit the display to upright plants. Bushy or trailing plants can be introduced if they will not be regularly brushed against. Cymbidium orchids make a dramatic impact in formal rooms, *Beaucarnea recurvata* are good in modern interiors, and an *Adiantum* (maidenhair fern) is compatible with most schemes. Combined with several treasured objects and planted in carefully chosen containers, these create an attractive still life that needs only a lamp to highlight the collection at night.

A group of low-level plants, such as *Soleirolia soleirolii*, *Nertera granadensis* or *Saintpaulia* (African violet), arranged together in one shallow basket or ceramic bowl, is perfect on a coffee table where it will be viewed from above. Putting all the plants in one container makes it more convenient if they need to be moved temporarily. A central dining table needs plants that are attractive from all sides. *Aglaonema* have large spear-shaped leaves which splay out to create a rounded, bushy shape. The green varieties can survive in fairly dim lighting,

*RIGHT Vigorous
climbers will form
an attractive focal
point in a room. The
plant can be trained
up a simple trellis
made from lengths of
bamboo cane, and
the trailing branches
can be pruned or
trained around
other stems.*

but the more interesting variegated types need bright conditions in order to maintain their leaf markings. As an alternative, several small pots of miniature roses, *Exacum affine* (Persian violet) or primulas grouped together when the table is not in use can then be split up to form a pretty line of colour for a dinner or lunch party. Because these plants will be viewed at very close proximity, they need to be in perfect condition and may remain so only for a couple of weeks.

Plants seen at a distance are better able to carry imperfections, especially if they are arranged in a tight group. With a sensitive selection of colours and shapes, considerable impact can be made using relatively small, inexpensive plants. Choose a colour theme of, say, white and green where a *Dieffenbachia compacta* sets the height of the arrangement for a range of smaller, bushier plants such as *Tolmiea menziesii* (piggyback plant), *Syngonium* and *Fittonia*. A trailing tradescantia will add a further dimension to the overall shape of the display, and a brilliant white azalea, *Argyranthemum frutescens* (marguerite) or scented gardenia will provide seasonal interest and variation. The success of these loose, informal groupings relies on establishing a strong central theme. While they offer numerous possibilities of choice and presentation, it is important to remember that the permanent plants must share the same light and temperature requirements.

LEFT A two-tiered plant stand or étagère *holds a collection of summer flowering plants including* Pelargonium *(geranium),* Gypsophila *and* Argyranthemum frutescens *(marguerite). These plants can be replaced on a seasonal basis with, say, lilies and narcissi in spring, and pot chrysanthemums in autumn.*

Choosing plants for size and shape

CLIMBING PLANTS

Flowering

Bougainvillea

Gloriosa

Hoya bella

Ipomoea

Jasminum officinale

Jasminum polyanthum

Passiflora caerulea

Plumbago auriculata

Stephanotis floribunda

Thunbergia alata

All-green and variegated

Fatshedera lizei

Hedera heliz

Philodendron scandens

Rhoicissus rhomboidea

Kalanchoe manginii

Schefflera

Scindapsus

Tetrastigma voinierianum

TRAILING PLANTS

Flowering

Acalpha hispida

Campanula isophylla

Columnea

Fuchsia

Kalanchoe manginii

Lantana camara

Osteospermum

Pelargonium peltatum

Torenia fournieri

All-green and variegated

Asparagus densiflorus

Callisia

Chlorophytum

Ficus pumila

Hedera helix

Nephrolepis

Plectranthus

Bougainvillea

Rhoicissus rhomboidea

Saxifraga stolonifera

Scindapsus

Sedum

Tolmiea menziesii

Tradescantia

LARGE-SCALE PLANTS

All-green and variegated

Araucaria heterophylla

Chamaedorea elegans

Chamaerops humilis

Chrysalidocarpus lutescens

Cocos nucifera

Cocos nucifera

Cupressus macrocarpa

Cycas revoluta

Cyperus

Dizygotheca elegantissima

Dracaena

Euphorbia

Fatshedera lizei

Fatsia japonica

Ficus benjamina

Ficus elastica

Ficus lyrata

Monstera deliciosa

Pachypodium

Philodendron

Phoenix canariensis

Radermachera

Schefflera

Syngonium

Yucca

Flowering

Bougainvillea

Jasminum officinale

Jasminum polyanthum

Sparmannia africana

SMALL-SCALE PLANTS

All-green and variegated

Acorus gramineus

Begonia boweri

Bonsai

Callisia

Coleus blumei

Fittonia

Hypoestes

Peperomia

Pilea

Selaginella

Soleirolia soleirolii

Varieties of Pilea

Flowering

Acalypha hispida

Achimenes hybrida

Begonia elatior

Beloperone guttata

Browallia

Campanula isophylla

Celosia

Chrysanthemum

Crocus

Cyclamen

Dahlia

Dianthus

Dionaea muscipula

Echeveria

Erica

Exacum affine

Hyacinthus

Kalanchoe

Nertera granadensis

Oxalis

Primula

Rosa

Saintpaulia

Streptocarpus

Varieties of Ficus benjamina

Creating Colour and Form

*P*rofessional designers have long valued the decorative qualities of plants, and use carefully selected plants to enhance and complement a specific theme. Just as importantly, indoor plants keep us in contact with nature, which is particularly important for city dwellers, who are rarely able to enjoy the therapeutic advantages of owning a garden.

ABOVE The brightly coloured leaves of Coleus blumei blend with hot, sunny colour schemes or add contrast to rooms decorated in shades of blue.

COLOUR NOTES

Although the vast majority of indoor plants are predominantly green, the choice of colour, shape and form is huge and diverse. The dramatic dark green foliage and shape of *Ficus lyrata* has a completely different look to that of the soft, lime green, vine-like leaves of a *Sparmannia africana* (houselime). The size

of the plant or plants and the density of colour need to be taken into account too – a roomful of plants is a striking colour scheme in itself, whereas one small basket of brightly coloured flowering plants will add a modest accent of colour picked up from furnishing accessories such as curtains and lampshades.

White and cream flowers and foliage are cool and soothing, and can also enhance a formal and sophisticated interior. A brilliant white *Phalaenopsis* (moth orchid) or cymbidium orchid will have a completely different impact to a group of white begonias; even though the colour is the same, it is the shape of the plant that makes the difference. Bright orange and vibrant yellow are cheerful, energizing colours, and a long, narrow planter filled with *Calendula* (marigold) and trailing *Tropaeolum majus* (nasturtium) makes a dynamic addition to a sunny kitchen windowsill. Flame-coloured *Coleus* combined with *Kalanchoe manginii* blend with yellow colour schemes and add a bright touch of contrast to rooms decorated in shades of blue.

In a hot, sunny room with plentiful bright light, the intense colours of the Mediterranean – Aegean blue, burnt orange, cerise and turquoise – demand a

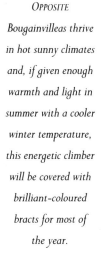

OPPOSITE Bougainvilleas thrive in hot sunny climates and, if given enough warmth and light in summer with a cooler winter temperature, this energetic climber will be covered with brilliant-coloured bracts for most of the year.

range of flowering plants in equally strong colours. *Pelargonium* (geranium) relish a hot, sunny climate, and this is also the only environment suited to bougainvillea. Glorious pink, crimson or purple bracts will cover this energetic climber, as long as it is baked in summer and kept cool in winter. *Gloriosa rothschildiana* (glory lily) is another sun lover, and can be trained to climb a mossed spike or trellis. It is a member of the lily family, and it has superb red flowers with recurved petals and bright yellow splayed stamens. It will flower from late spring and continue throughout the summer.

When summer is over, flowering houseplants provide much-needed natural colour throughout autumn and winter. The range of all-year-round plants offers scope for experimenting with colour. Just as a vase of cut flowers using one

ABOVE LEFT Azaleas and poinsettias are popular choices for winter colour.

ABOVE RIGHT Foliage and flowers have been chosen to match a wallpaper and fabric – Hedera helix *(common ivy),* Streptocarpus, Begonia rex *and* Maranta leuconeura.

variety or colour makes a focal point, a group of bright blue *Campanula* (bell-flower) or crimson azaleas has the same effect, with the advantage that they last longer. When they are past their best, be ruthless and throw or give them away. Constantly refreshing interiors with plants in different colours keeps decorative schemes lively and interesting.

ROOM STYLES, PLANT STYLES

Stark architectural interiors which are typified by plain materials, little or no pattern and monochromatic colours need strong, linear plant forms such as specimen *Howea forsteriana* (kentia palm), *Cocos nucifera* (coconut palm) and *Yucca elephantipes* (spineless yucca). These plants have a deep green, glossy foliage that complements polished black leather sofas and gleaming chrome-framed chairs. These immaculate and austere interiors need beautifully maintained plants to provide the perfect living sculptures that this style of room demands. Use commercial leaf shine to keep the leaves shiny, or mix some water with a little milk and wipe the leaves with a soft cloth to produce the same effect.

Small rooms will appear visually larger if they are simply furnished and kept uncluttered. Japanese-style interiors have plain and neutral colours and simple shapes, and the minimal furniture tends to be small and low-level. In such a set-ting large dominant plants would be over-powering. *Bambusa vulgaris* (common bamboo), with its delicate leaves, is an authentic choice, and this plant has recently been adapted for indoor cultiva-tion. Several small bonsai are also in keeping with a Japanese-style decor. These dwarf trees need plenty of bright light in order to thrive, and prefer an east- or west-facing windowsill. If you find this oriental simplicity rather too aus-tere, however, try softening it with small quantities of bright colour such as sharp pink or sunshine yellow.

Other trends in interior schemes include those based on the rich, earthy tones and patterns found in fabrics, car-pets and ornaments from India, Indonesia and Africa. Such schemes are comple-mented by the colours and shapes of many semi-tropical and tropical plants such as *Ananas bracteatus striatus* (red pineapple), *Codiaeum*, *Maranta* and the numerous bromeliads, all of which are exotically striped and patterned. Contained in simple terracotta pots, they will enhance any ethnic-style room.

COUNTRY STYLE

The loose, informal country style is one of the most important decorative influ-ences of the nineties. The desire to bring the garden into the home has seen the creation of scores of new floral fabrics and furnishings, as well as the revival of numerous traditional chintz designs. Bold

ABOVE A modern interior with a strong colour theme is enhanced by a collection of all-green plants.

LEFT Containers such as kitchen pots and jugs help to create an informal country feel.

Weathered terracotta, loosely woven baskets and faded china cachepots make sympathetic containers for both flowering and foliage plants. A room decorated with delicate pinks and creams and furnished with plump, chintz-covered sofas is made even more attractive by the addition of a large basket of plants that change with the seasons. Try fragrant pink hyacinth in spring and tiny rose bushes in summer, followed by daisy-shaped autumnal chrysanthemum and miniature cyclamen in winter.

In traditional country- and rustic-style homes, permanent plants with small, rounded leaves look best. *Ficus pumila*

OPPOSITE Tulips have an elegant formality and, with such a range of varieties, there is a shade to match or add impact to every colour scheme.

BELOW Hydrangea macrophylla has naturally pink flowers which turn blue when watered with aluminium sulphate.

ABOVE A very relaxed country style is created with tall, small-leaved and rambling plants, such as ivies, ferns and vines, which may be left to trail or can be trained up a trellis or stick.

checks and stripes printed on thick, rough cotton and linen are also applied to rugs, wall tiles and china to evoke the simplicity of English country cottages or French Provençal farmhouses of old. Hand-crafted furniture with original vernacular detailing, constructed from indigenous woods such as beech, oak and cherry provide natural, not to say ecologically friendly, colour and texture. A sensitive use of colour and shape when it comes to plants and their containers is essential in order to complete this easy, restful style.

rounded leaves edged with bright pink. It produces tiny platelets at the ends of numerous runners. These plants look attractive trailing from a sunny window-sill, mantelpiece or shelf.

For a more dramatic impact, a large flowering plant such as *Hydrangea macrophylla* is a delightful addition in summer. Hydrangeas come in so many shades of pink that it is possible to match exactly the tones in a pink colour scheme or even a specific fabric.

TREES FOR STYLE

Red and pink are the most common colours of *Rhododendron simsii*, and the species is available in numerous shapes and sizes. A recent addition is the standard azalea, which resembles a standard bay tree in shape. It has one tall, thin trunk about 1 m (3 ft) high with a bushy mop-shaped top covered with rich green leaves and a mass of flowers. This compact shape atop its narrow upright form has a pleasing formality. A pair could be placed either side of French windows or at either end of a sofa. Another popular standard tree available in spring and summer is *Argyranthemum frutescens* (marguerite). These plants are grown to heights of 1–1.2 m (3 ft–3 ft 10 in) and their dome-shaped foliage can be as much as 1.2 m (3 ft 10 in) in diameter. They are covered with white- or cream-coloured daisies with yellow centres, and make a very refreshing addition to any room with a bright position.

(creeping fig) is a climbing plant but could trail if stood on a tall plant stand. These plants have pretty heart-shaped leaves and many are variegated with white spots or cream edges. Or try the rambling climber *Hedera helix* (common ivy), which also lends an air of soft informality. *Fittonia* is a ground creeper originating from Peru and its mid-green leaves are covered with scores of white veins. Several plants massed in a low

ceramic container provide a living pattern that complements delicate floral designs. *Hypoestes* has coloured veining but also bright splodges of pink, white or dark red, and several varieties planted together make more impact than a single plant. *Hypoestes* generally last for about a year before they lose their compact shape and their distinctive markings start to fade. An easier and longer-lasting plant is *Saxifraga stolonifera* 'Tricolor', which has

Choosing plants for colour

WHITE/CREAM FLOWERS	YELLOW FLOWERS	ORANGE/RED FLOWERS
Anthurium	*Acacia*	*Abutilon*
Begonia elatior	*Allamanda cathartica*	*Acalypha hispida*
Browallia	*Aphelandra squarrosa*	*Achimenes hybrida*
Campanula	*Begonia elatior*	*Anthurium*
Chrysanthemum	*Chrysanthemum*	*Begonia elatior*
Citrus mitis	*Crocus*	*Calathea*
Clerodendrum	*Cymbidium*	*Celosia*
Crocus	*Cytisus*	*Chrysanthemum*
Cyclamen	*Echeveria*	*Columnea*
Cymbidium	*Gerbera*	*Cyclamen persicum*
Euphorbia milii	*Hibiscus*	*Cymbidium*
Euphorbia pulcherrima	*Kalanchoe*	*Dianthus*
Eustoma grandiflorum	*Lilium*	*Euphorbia pulcherrima*
Exacum affine	*Narcissus*	*Gerbera*
Gardenia	*Pachystachys lutea*	*Gloriosa*
Hibiscus	*Rosa*	*Guzmania*
Hippeastrum	*Tulipa*	*Hibiscus*
Hoya bella		*Hippeastrum*
Hyacinthus		*Impatiens*
Hydrangea		*Kalanchoe*
Jasminum officinale		*Lilium*
Lilium		*Nertera granadensis*
Narcissus		*Pelargonium*
Nerium oleander		*Primula*
Oxalis		*Rhipsalidopsis gaertneri*
Phalaenopsis		*Rhododendron simsii*
Rhododendron simsii		*Rosa*
Rosa		*Schizanthus retusus*
Saintpaulia		*Sinningia*
Sinningia		*Tulipa*
Spathiphyllum		*Vriesea*
Stephanotis floribunda		*Zantedeschia*
Zantedeschia		*Zygocactus truncatus*

Rosa chinensis minima

PINK FLOWERS

Achimenes hybrida
Aechmea fasciata
Anthurium
Astilbe arendsii
Begonia elatior
Beloperone guttata
Bougainvillea
Callistephus
Chrysanthemum
Clerodendrum
Cyclamen persicum
Cymbidium
Dahlia
Dianthus
Erica
Euphorbia pulcherrima
Eustoma grandiflorum
Fuchsia
Gerbera
Hibiscus
Hippeastrum
Hyacinthus
Impatiens
Kalanchoe
Lilium
Nerium oleander
Oxalis
Pelargonium
Primula
Rhipsalidopsis gaertneri
Rhododendron simsii
Rosa
Saintpaulia
Tillandsia lindenii
Tulipa
Zantedeschia

Campanula isophylla

LILAC-PURPLE FLOWERS

Bougainvillea
Chrysanthemum
Crocus
Eustoma grandiflorum
Exacum affine
Plumbago indica
Primula
Saintpaulia
Sinningia

BLUE FLOWERS

Achimenes hybrida
Browallia
Brunfelsia
Campanula
Crocus
Hyacinthus
Hydrangea
Ipomoea
Muscari
Passiflora caerulea
Saintpaulia
Scilla sibirica
Senecio cruentus

VARIEGATED AND COLOURED FOLIAGE

Acorus gramineus
Aglaonema
Ananas
Aphelandra
Begonia boweri
Caladium
Calathea
Callisia
Chlorophytum
Codiaeum
Coleus
Cordyline
Dieffenbachia
Dracaena
Euonymus
Fatshedera lizei
Fatsia
Ficus benjamina
Ficus pumila
Fittonia
Hedera helix
Hypoestes
Maranta
Monstera deliciosa
Peperomia
Pilea
Sansevieria
Saxifraga
Schefflera
Scindapsus
Sedum
Tradescantia
Vriesea
Yucca
Zebrina

Making the Most of Scent

ABOVE A window box brimming with scented Pelargonium *(geranium) and creeping thyme is positioned where people will brush past the leaves, releasing their delicate fragrance.*

The fact that no single plant will flower all year round should not be seen as a limitation, but rather as a marvellous opportunity to introduce different scents according to the season to maintain fragrance from spring through to winter.

On a practical note, generally, if a flowering plant is refusing or reluctant to flower, it is probably not getting enough light. The remedy is to reposition it in a place that receives more intense light for a longer period each day.

SCENT THROUGH THE YEAR

Spring is probably the easiest season, and offers numerous varieties of scented narcissi and hyacinths that are ideal for growing indoors. Individual pots of hyacinths planted at fortnightly intervals in autumn give a continuity of scent throughout spring for very little cost.

Summer too offers an enormous choice of fragrant shrubs and plants. Bouvardia has gained in popularity as a cut flower, and is also available as an indoor flowering plant. It is quite a difficult specimen to grow and it will only last a few years, but its scented flowers appear in summer and continue through to early winter. Far easier to grow are the numerous varieties of aromatic

OPPOSITE Individual pots of hyacinths planted at two- or three-week intervals in the autumn will give a continuous scented display throughout the spring.

$\mathcal{N}$o garden would be complete without scented flowers and shrubs, and by far the most popular flowers are those with a distinctive perfume: roses, sweet peas, tobacco plants, lilacs, lavender and freesias. Outdoors you need either large beds of these flowers to pervade the air with scent or specially constructed arbours for climbing roses or honeysuckle. In a confined space, a single scented plant is often all it takes to fill a room with a heady perfume, which may be delightful to some but cloying and overpowering to others. To make sure you are happy with your choice, buy plants as they are just coming into bloom, as this is both a guarantee that they will blossom, and an opportunity to check that you like their perfume.

RIGHT Jasminum officinale *and pots of* Nicotiana *grown near a balcony door exude a heady perfume from late afternoon in the summer months.*

Pelargonium (geranium) that start flowering in late spring and, given a warm and sunny windowsill, will carry on well into autumn. Their fragrance is light and delicate and you will need several plants for their scent to make an impact. Choose a sill where people regularly brush past, as the scent is held in the leaves of the plant. *Pelargonium* grow wild all over the Mediterranean region, where they relish a poor soil and hot sun. *Nerium oleander* (oleander) enjoy the same climate, and these dense, bushy shrubs produce white, pink, red and yellow fragrant flowers nearly all year. In cooler climates, oleander may only flower at the height of the

growing season, and only then if they are given a hot sunny position. One word of warning: oleander are highly poisonous and should not be kept in an apartment where children are living. All parts of the plant are toxic and you need to wash your hands every time you touch them. The same caution should be applied to the stunning but poisonous *Datura candida* (angel's trumpet). Its flared, trumpet-shaped flowers can measure up to 20 cm (8 in) in length and hang downwards between very attractive oval leaves.

For a concentrated perfume in summer there is nothing more potent than lilies. The wonderful intensity of their fragrance

increases from late afternoon into evening and is matched by their exotically beautiful flowers. Specially prepared lily bulbs can be grown in winter and their planting staggered to give flowers from summer into autumn. Not all lilies are fragrant, however. As a general guide, the mid-century hybrid varieties, which are generally cheaper than the perfumed kinds, have bright colours but no scent. *Lilium longiflorum* (Easter lily), *L. regale* and many of the *L. speciosum* (Japanese lily) varieties, on the other hand, have such a heady scent that two or three plants are all that are needed. These lilies are also available as fully mature potted plants virtually all year round, and, as the flowers can last from between three to four weeks if bought in bud, they are a viable alternative to buying cut stems. When buying the mature plants, always choose ones with healthy green foliage and lots of fat, coloured buds. Keep the compost damp – a thick mulch of moss is both a decorative soil cover and helps to retain moisture. High humidity and a cool temperature will dramatically lengthen the life of the flowers. After flowering, if you keep the plants until the foliage has shrivelled, the bulbs can be repotted for the following year or put out into a friend's garden.

If the general atmosphere of the apartment is very warm throughout the summer, you may find it easy to keep a *Jasminum officinale* or a *Stephanotis floribunda*. These vigorous climbers love heat

MAKING THE MOST OF SCENT

LEFT A sweet mixture of perfumed Lilium longiflorum, planted in pots, form the centrepiece of this exotic display, and are surrounded by the scented cut flowers of freesias, Polianthes tuberosa, Lathyrus odoratus (sweet pea), and Stephanotis floribunda.

and humidity when in flower, but prefer a cooler temperature during the winter when they are resting. Make sure they have a permanent position, as neither plant likes being moved and may respond

by refusing to flower. As with so many other semi-tropical and tropical flowering plants, a warm and humid conservatory is the only real guarantee of successful cultivation. If you do not have a

conservatory, settle for smaller plants that can be enjoyed for the weeks they are in flower and then discarded.

Gardenia jasminoides is another notoriously difficult plant to maintain. It demands high temperatures and humidity to flower, but when it does it has soft, creamy white flowers with an intense perfume out of proportion to their size. This is one plant where commercial growers have deliberately concentrated their efforts in increasing the flower's scent. A recent introduction are the double-shaped varieties, which have a sensational fragrance. Always buy these plants in flower and avoid touching their petals, which bruise easily and then turn brown. They need a brightly lit position and at least 18°C (65°F) in a humid atmosphere throughout the summer to flower successfully; during their resting period in winter the temperature must drop to at least 12°C (54°F) if they are to stand any chance of flowering again. A south-facing bathroom windowsill (north-facing in the Southern hemisphere) is an ideal position. Even without flowers, gardenia have attractive shiny, dark-green foliage.

Orange blossom has a delicious fragrance, and dwarf citrus trees are being bred by crossing *Fortunella margarita* (kumquats) with either lemon or lime trees. These have tiny, fragrant white flowers which subsequently develop into small oranges. These are edible if extremely bitter tasting. Fruit will not be forthcoming, however, unless the orange tree either has a period outdoors to pollinate naturally in summer or you transfer pollen using a very fine brush if the plant has to be confined indoors. Trees such as

Citrus mitis are cultivated to grow to around 1 m (3 ft) in height, but orange trees home-grown from sowing the pips may grow a great deal higher, although they rarely develop flowers or fruit.

Another summer-flowering plant that has gained in popularity in recent years is *Exacum affine* (Persian violet). Commercial growers have developed new hybrids which produce carpets of tiny purple or white scented flowers, resembling those of the *Saintpaulia* (African violet) plant. *E. affine* has a rounded bushy growth that makes it a good shape for putting three or four plants together in a low container where the plants can be seen all the way around. The plants will tend to thrive better in such an arrangement, as *E. affine* prefer a humid atmosphere, and a group of plants will always retain moisture more readily than a plant on its own.

ABOVE Narcissus tazetta *have small flowers which are usually scented – in particular the varieties 'Soleil d'Or' and 'Paperwhite'.*

E. affine will bloom all summer long if given a fortnightly feed, a brightly lit position and fairly damp compost. Frequent dead heading also encourages new flowers to appear.

Rosa chinensis, the miniature rose tree, also flowers in summer. Until recently they have been cultivated mainly for their tiny size and profuse flowering, but, as with many other commercially grown roses, breeders are now developing scented hybrids. The popularity of scented varieties has affected production of the dwarf *Cyclamen persicum* too. The original species has a very slight but pleasant scent, which is now being bred back into some of the miniature varieties.

Choosing plants for scent

LIGHT FRAGRANCES

Bouvardia longiflorum

Cyclamen persicum (miniature)

Datura candida

Dianthus

Hoya bella

Hymenocallis x festalis

Hymenocallis narcissiflora

Nerium oleander

Rosa chinensis

Stephanotis floribunda

NAMED SCENTS

Citrus mitis – orange

Exacum affine – violet

Pelargonium blandfordianum
   – almond

Pelargonium capitatum – rose

Pelargonium crispum – lemon

Pelargonium fragrans – citrus

Pelargonium graveolens – rose

Pelargonium odoratissimum
   – lemon

Pelargonium quercifolium
   –camphor

Pelargonium tomentosum – mint

HEAVY PERFUMES

Datura suaveolens

Freesia

Gardenia jasminoides

Hyacinthus

Jasminum officinale

Jasminum polyanthum

Lavandula

Lilium (oriental hybrids)

Narcissus

Stephanotis floribunda

Nerium oleander

Citrus mitis

Stylish Containers

*E*nthusiastic indoor gardeners are always looking for new ideas and novel ways of presenting their plants. Fortunately, there are almost no limits as to what you can use as the containers, but the most effective ideas rely on a harmonious relationship between the container, plant and the environment in which they are placed. Your choice of container will inevitably affect the appearance of a plant as well as the style and mood of the room; a beautifully designed interior can so easily be spoilt by a collection of ill-fitting and ill-matching planters, even if the plants themselves are extremely attractive. Since the sixties, when plastic planters in stark, artificial colours were all the vogue, there has been a gradual but positive shift towards pot holders made of wicker and bamboo, muted terra-cotta, putty toned clay, subtly stained wood and brightly coloured and often hand-painted ceramics. Many garden centres and plant specialists also sell a range of planters and baskets so that plants and pots can conveniently be bought together. If you have a favourite container, take it along with you when choosing plants and try out several different shapes and sizes until you find the perfect match.

OPPOSITE Brushed steel, shiny chrome and wire baskets contrast with lush green foliage and look effective in cool, modern interiors.

RIGHT Glazed ceramics offer a wide choice of colour and pattern, and designs can be selected to match exactly both foliage and flowers.

Small, bushy plants generally look best in containers that approximately match their size or are slightly smaller. A tall, thin plant, say 24 cm (10 in) to 60 cm (2 ft) high, will be better balanced in a pot that is roughly a quarter its height. Of course, this is only a general guide, but, as a rule, the bigger the plant, the smaller the pot should be in relationship to it. Although aesthetics play an important role when choosing a container, it must also be heavy enough, and therefore large enough, to provide a solid base; otherwise, if the soil dries out, the plant could easily topple over.

BASKETS

Containers need not be expensive. Baskets are cheap and make one of the most versatile choices. Many baskets are designed specifically to hold plants, but waste paper baskets, hampers and log baskets can all be used for large specimens. A pot-shaped basket is ideal for individual plants, while a basket with a handle is useful for climbing varieties and also trailing plants as the basket can be lifted and turned without disturbing the leaves and branches that are spilling over the rim. A mixed arrangement of small flowering or green plants makes an

impact on low surfaces when it is displayed in a wide, shallow basket. Lined with plastic and with a layer of crocks, the plants can be transplanted directly into the basket or left in their individual pots, the rims concealed with moss or a thin layer of soil or stones.

The natural tones of baskets made from bamboo, wicker, raffia and willow are perfect for relaxed, comfortable and country-style apartments. Toning colour can be added with spray paints either to form an overall colour or to create patterns such as bands, stripes and delicate stencilled designs.

The one disadvantage of baskets is that they are not watertight, although this problem is easily addressed. The insides can be lined with strong plastic sheeting cut to size and either sewn or wired securely just below the internal edge. As an alternative, select a basket that is big enough to take a plant, its plastic pot and drip tray. Placing the drip tray under the basket does not look very attractive, and is not practical either as the basket will eventually rot. An old ceramic pot which fits snugly at the base of the basket is better than a saucer, which may overflow, and the additional weight of the bowl will also keep the plant more stable. Make sure that the inner plant pot sits below the rim of the basket so that the dark surface of the soil is out of view and does not detract from the display.

Be careful never to overwater plants in baskets, and always protect the surface

RIGHT Glass pots and tanks can be lined with coloured stones, a thick layer of moss or – as shown here with this Pteris cretica *(ribbon fern) – transparent glass marbles.*

on which they are standing. Ideally, you should water a basket on a waterproof top such as a draining board or in a bath where excess water can run away without causing any damage.

TERRACOTTA

Large terracotta pots are good containers for large specimens, as their weight gives stability for thin trunks with wide arching branches. If a plant needs to be moved outside during the summer months, a clay pot can withstand rain and shine and its appearance will even improve with a degree of weathering. For plants that need humidity, select a drip tray large enough to take the plant pot with space for stones or water-retaining granules. Raise the plant pot on terracotta "feet" (available at good garden centres) or use an upturned smaller terracotta drip tray. Match the drip tray to the style of the pot, but make sure that it is internally glazed or water will seep through.

In its natural state terracotta blends in with most interiors, and the rather severe orange tone of brand new terracotta can be softened by leaving it outside for the winter on a patio or balcony. It can also be artificially aged by rubbing in a weak solution of pale water-based paint. You might also like to try various special paint techniques on it such as sponging, dragging and stencilling. Interest can be added by searching out for pots embossed with patterns or motifs, and with decorative handles or fluted rims.

TOP Baskets make excellent plant holders. If they are lined with plastic, plants can be transplanted directly into the basket.

ABOVE Terracotta has a warm colouring which blends with most interiors. Colour may also be added with water-based paint or stencils.

ABOVE For spring, a glass cylinder is planted with hyacinth bulbs grown in water. The bulbs rest on large pebbles so that the roots reach down to the water below.

CERAMICS

Glazed ceramic containers offer a wide choice in terms of colours and patterns, and designs can be chosen to match foliage and flowers as well as the interior decoration. Pots in solid tones are generally more versatile than patterned ones, and can be used to make the visual link between the room's colour scheme and the plants' foliage. Use a group of similarly decorated pots for a collection of compatible plants and periodically double

them up as vases for cut flowers and foliage. Most ceramic containers will not have a drainage hole, so make sure that the inner pot can be easily lifted out for watering or that it rests on a bed of crocks so that excess water does not remain in contact with the base of the inner pot (this can cause the plant's roots to rot). If the ceramic container has a drainage hole, choose one with a matching drip tray rather than resorting to an ill-matching saucer.

ABOVE In summer, the same glass container is planted with a highly scented Stephanotis floribunda, which is surrounded by stones to conceal the plastic inner pot.

ABOVE For autumn, a pot of perfumed 'Stargazer' lilies is covered with layers of seasonal pine cones and dried chilli peppers to tone with the deep red spots and markings on the petals.

EVERYDAY CONTAINERS

Household objects such as old bowls, lidless casseroles, soup tureens and even large mugs or teapots can make unusual containers. Decorated metalware such as large olive-oil or coffee tins would be appropriate in a kitchen, for instance, and even a plastic pot is acceptable if covered in some way, perhaps with some fabric from a room's soft furnishings.

Glass containers offer a further dimension to traditional pots, as the plants may be surrounded with pebbles, gravel or sand. For a particularly decorative finish, use a mixture of pretty stones and seashells. Take two glass pots that will fit one inside the other so that there is a thin gap between the two that can be filled with either pot pourri, aromatic herbs and spices, or layers of coloured sand or bath crystals. If the plant inside needs a high degree of humidity, fill the gap with coloured gravel or tiny stones and keep it topped up with water.

ABOVE Pots of winter-flowering Primula acaulis (primrose) are raised on a bed of sand and stones. A layer of gravel conceals the topsoil of their pots and also prevents excessive water loss.

Decorating terracotta pots

Cheap terracotta pots can be made into highly decorative and distinctive containers with the addition of some simple stencilled designs. Choose paints to enhance the flowers or foliage of the plant you wish to display, or to match a colour scheme. Terracotta is quite porous and may need more than one or two coats of paint, depending on the colour.

1 To follow this project you will need a clean terracotta pot, a tape measure, a piece of chalk, a ruler, water-based or acrylic paints in various colours, stencil brushes, plastic stencils and masking tape.

2 Divide the pot into equal sections using the tape measure, and mark each one with chalk.

3 Mark the outlines of the shapes and paint within the outlines. Allow to dry.

4 Attach the stencil to the pot with masking tape, then apply several coats of paint.

5 Move the stencil to the rim of the pot and repeat the process.

LEFT Once you have gained some confidence with simple stencils, experiment with freehand designs and sponging, stippling and dragging techniques. Try using other types of paint, too, such as metallics.

Gardens within Gardens

*M*ost indoor gardeners soon discover that they have a definite preference for a particular group of plants. It may be that they like the shape or colour of the leaves or simply that they are very successful at growing that variety of plant – always a satisfying experience for any gardener. Some of the most popular indoor plant collections include herbs, cacti and succulents, and fabulous orchids.

Keen cooks relish the opportunity to use fresh herbs to flavour recipes and to garnish plates and dishes with bright leaves, and a number of herbs are easy to grow indoors. A parsley pot is a practical

BELOW Many plants are available in miniature sizes. A collection may be started to see which plants thrive best, before investing in the full-size, more expensive specimens.

way of growing windowsill herbs. It is usually made from terracotta, and it is perforated with numerous open "pockets" for planting out small plants or seeds of parsley, as well as bush basil, creeping thyme and marjoram. Seedlings are recommended so that the pot does not remain bare while the seeds germinate. Some plants, such as parsley, are notoriously difficult to start off from seed, and in most cases seedlings will guarantee uniform growth. Pots of mint, sage, thyme, chives, rosemary and bay will grow on sunny window ledges both inside and out; they need regular picking to keep their shape, so choose varieties that will be used regularly. Basil and parsley are usually required in large quantities to flavour sauces and salads – grow them in big pots to keep pace with demand. Small pots of aromatic herbs, on the other hand, make attractive table decorations both for inside and for summer meals on the balcony or patio.

THE EXOTIC GARDEN

A sunny windowsill is the ideal environment for a magnificent collection of cacti and succulents. Their natural habitat is the American prairies and desert regions, and they demand a potting medium that

OPPOSITE A variety of herbs close at hand in the kitchen adds zest and flavour to cooking. Butchers' hooks are used to suspend wire baskets from a painted trellis to give the plants the maximum light from the window.

resembles desert sand. Commercially prepared cactus soil, which provides a free-draining and well-aerated medium, is available from garden centres; it can also be mixed with additional sand. Add a top layer of pretty stones for a more attractive presentation. In summer, cacti can be watered quite regularly, but never leave them standing in water. In autumn they should be given only a little water, and none at all during the winter months when they are resting.

Forest cacti are known for their attractive flowers, which appear to sprout from the leaf – actually a flattened stem. *Epiphyllum* hybrids are the most

ABOVE Vriesea splendens, Tillandsia lindenii *and* Guzmania lingulata major *are all bromeliads which prefer a humid environment.*

spectacular, with large, fragrant blooms. Also popular are *Rhipsalidopsis gaertneri* (Easter cactus), which flowers in early to late spring, and *Zygocactus truncatus* (Christmas cactus), which blooms in early to mid-winter. A display combining these two varieties would give two long-lasting flowering seasons a year. To stimulate flower development, both plants benefit from spending a couple of months outdoors during the summer. Although they require bright light, they must also be protected from full sunlight. Also be sure to safeguard them from slugs. While they are outdoors, fill the vacant windowsill position with some summer-flowering pot plants such as pansies, petunias or even tomatoes. Unlike most houseplants, cacti and succulents need more specialized care if they are to reach their full potential

ABOVE Perennial herbs such as sage, chives and thyme will grow quite happily on a sunny windowsill and will only need reporting once a year.

and flower. They inevitably appeal to the indoor gardener who has the time and interest to develop a collection of more demanding varieties.

Orchids also need specialist care. These fascinating and exotic plants include around 30,000 species with more than 70,000 hybrids. With the exception of desert and sub-zero regions, orchids grow all over the world, mainly in the Asiatic regions and in Central and South America, although there are some orchids that are native to Europe. Prized for their sensational flowers, orchids need careful attention all year round to ensure success. Re-creating their native habitats is essential, and a temperature-controlled sun room or conservatory is advisable if a collection is both to grow and expand. Cymbidium hybrids are one of the most popular and easiest varieties to grow indoors. Their popularity is mainly due to the longevity of their flowers, which bloom in an incredible range of colours, markings, shapes and sizes. Lots of light, a high level of humidity and specialized compost and feeding are essential. To flourish, they also need warmth during the day in summer and cool, fresh air at night, particularly prior to flowering – conditions that are not always readily available in apartments.

THE LOW-MAINTENANCE GARDEN

Rather than struggle with a plant whose natural habitat is difficult to maintain, many indoor gardeners find it more rewarding to collect a variety that is happy to share its preferred environment. If ferns or palms thrive in a particular room, expand on that group and investigate other plant possibilities from specialist nurseries and growers. Begonias are very easy plants to grow and merely require bright light and a constant warm environment that never falls below about 16°C (61°F), which is a reasonable year-round room temperature. There are scores of beautifully patterned and coloured leaf begonias, many of which also come into flower. They are simple to propagate from leaf and root cuttings,

and the plants are easy to divide at the potting on stage, so you can make presents of new plants to friends and family as well as swapping cuttings with other begonia collectors.

An alternative to sharing your environment with plants is to create a mini climate within a bottle or terrarium. A terrarium is easier to maintain than a bottle, as the plants may be pruned or removed merely by lifting the lid of the terrarium, and therefore a wider choice of species can be planted and replaced when they have faded. *Selaginella*, *Fittonia* and *Hypoestes* make attractive ground

cover, with a couple of ferns or palms for height and miniature flowering plants such as gloxinia or *Exacum* added for seasonal colour. Given good light and a constant, warm temperature, the necessary humid environment required in a terrarium is maintained by the moisture given off the plants' leaves condensing and returning to the soil, ready to start the watering cycle again.

BELOW A large, sunny window provides the perfect spot for a collection of cacti and succulents. These plants need regular watering in summer and none at all during the winter.

A GARDEN
IN EVERY ROOM

Every room in your apartment may provide a different
microclimate for plants – ferns and shade-loving
varieties in the bathroom, herbs in the kitchen for
instant relishes, ever-changing seasonal colour for
living spaces, and light fragrances in the bedrooms.

Living Rooms

For many of us, the living room is the space where we express most our personality, style and taste. It is the room most frequently presented to the outside world, and it is also the place where we can relax in privacy and comfort. By choosing and displaying foliage and flowering plants in an imaginative way, you can enhance the atmosphere and style of this important living area.

As comfort is a top priority in most living rooms, there will inevitably be low surfaces in close proximity to seating and these are obvious sites for plants. The danger here is, of course, that they can very easily take over all the available space, leaving nowhere for cups, glasses and magazines. To avoid this problem, select a large, low container that can hold a group of plants and is roomy enough to prevent the plants ever getting out of hand. Plants grouped together not only make more of a statement, but their close proximity also increases humidity. Select plants that like similar light conditions and have the same watering requirements. It is much easier to remember to water them at the same time each week than have a complicated rota when inevitably some will be neglected by either over- or underwatering.

LEFT Primula obconica *is a delightful plant with clusters of pale blue flowers, but can cause an allergic reaction.*

OPPOSITE Sparmannia africana *(house lime) can grow to 6 m (18 ft) and needs annual pruning to maintain its shape.*

One major problem to look out for in living rooms is the effect of central heating on plants. Few tropical plants can tolerate dry heat, and the only way to get round this is to raise the amount of moisture there is in the air. The cheapest way to increase humidity levels is to place pots on trays covered with a layer of wet pebbles; the most costly is to use commercial room humidifiers. If a radiator has its own humidifier – a small, relatively inexpensive one hung from the top – and a shelf running along its length, this will be a suitable spot for plants, depending, of course, on the light levels. In summer when the heating is turned off

it could be a temporary home for seasonal flowers: perhaps a long basket of scented lilies, brightly coloured *Senecio cruentus* (cineraria) or outdoor bedding plants such as pansies, gerberas, *Eustoma* or dahlias.

If your living room has an adjoining space to the outside, this opens up a new area of possibilities for displaying plants. Many palms, for example, enjoy a summer holiday in the fresh air, and, if the balcony or patio is only used in summer, it is an economical way of furnishing it with plants before returning them to the living room in autumn. The time to bring them in is when it is too chilly to sit outside in the evenings.

LEFT Given a warm and humid environment with good indirect light, Saintpaulia (African violet) will flower virtually all year round and make a pretty, small-scale display.

lime), on the other hand, enjoys a rapid growth rate. Its increasing popularity can be attributed not just to its luxuriant growth but also to the soft colour and texture of its leaves, which blend harmoniously with neutral colour schemes.

LIVING COLOUR

Flowering plants are a wonderful way to bring living colour to an overall design. Just one vase of seasonal flowers can add that finishing touch to a living room, as can a bowl of bright blue hydrangeas or a basket full of brilliant cerise or pillar-box red azaleas. The main advantage of these pot plants over cut flowers is that they will still be flourishing long after the flower arrangement has faded. When the plants have stopped flowering, put them somewhere less prominent. There are some plants that will naturalize outside in a garden. Primulas or *Campanula* (bellflower), for instance, will survive planted out in a sheltered spot. A pot of *Muscari* (grape hyacinth), *Narcissus* 'Tête-à-Tête' or tulips can be repotted outside after flowering and brought in the following year as their shoots begin to show.

Exotic flowering plants add sophistication to a living space. Smaller cymbidium orchids are ideal for coffee tables, mantelpieces or shelves. Larger specimens need a

STRIKING GREENERY

Large specimen plants are always a popular choice for living rooms, as they provide a strong focal point in both traditional and contemporary interiors. The arching leaves of *Howea forsteriana* (kentia palm) form an elegant shape that suits almost any style of room, but remember that these palms can grow to between 2–3 m (6–9 ft) tall. Other palms such as *Chrysalidocarpus lutescens* (areca palm) and *Caryota mitis* reach a similar height when mature, and have tall stems that make their proportions ideal where floor space is restricted. These graceful plants promote a restful and relaxing atmosphere during the day; at night, strike a more dramatic note by placing

a few strategically placed uplighters so that their leaves form dramatic shadows on walls and ceilings.

Another large plant that enhances modern or simple interiors is *Dracaena marginata*. This plant has tall, snake-like trunk branches from which crowns of thin, arching leaves fan out in bushy clusters. The varieties *D. marginata* 'Tricolor' and *D. marginata* 'Colorama' have variegated leaves which add splashes of red and yellow-red to the plant. Yucca, with its fat woody stem and mop heads of sword-shaped leaves, also creates a strong angular presence.

Even under the right conditions, the plants described so far are still relatively slow growers. *Sparmannia africana* (house pedestal or plant stand so that their sensational flowers can be appreciated to the full. Another exotic plant that is usually bought in flower is *Anthurium scherzerianum*. It has pretty heart-shaped flowers coloured either red, pink or white and grows to about 30–35 cm (12–14 in) in height, making it ideal for low tables.

Variegated plants such as *Begonia rex* and *Coleus blumei* look very attractive grouped together, perhaps in a large container on a side table. Both these plants have showy leaves with distinctive patterns and markings in a range of pinks, reds and maroons – warm, welcoming colours that are frequently used in living rooms. Make sure that the container tones in with the plants. Circular shapes are ideal if the arrangement is to be seen from all sides, and this should be turned regularly so that all the plants benefit from the source of light.

ABOVE A tall, thin pedestal makes the most of the trailing habit of this bushy **Asparagus densiflorus,** *and can be turned easily to ensure even growth.*

LEFT **Chrysalidocarpus lutescens** *is a slow-growing palm, so it needs to be acquired at the height which will best suit the proportions of the room.*

RIGHT **Phyllostachys aureas** *(fishpole bamboo) is ideally placed by a full-length window and will live quite happily outside during the summer months.*

Dining Rooms

aking room in an apartment for a separate dining area is quite a luxury unless the kitchen is minute and impossible to eat in. Generally, the dining area forms part of the kitchen or living room, or indeed both. Often a separate dining room also doubles up as a study or spare bedroom, and its frequency of use will help decide on the type of plants best suited to it. Fortunately, there is a wide range of plants to choose from, including ferns, fragrant plants such as jasmine, and dramatic bromeliads.

ELEGANT GREENERY

A large *Nephrolepsis exaltata* (sword fern) may look fantastic in one corner of a dining room, but, if the heating is turned on only when the room is in use, it will not survive. Conversely, if the room is always hot and dry the fern will only be happy if given constant and high humidity by installing an electric humidifier, misting the fronds daily and setting the plant on a tray of pebbles that are continually kept wet. That is a great deal of care and maintenance for one fern! For the same effect and much less trouble, go for an *Arachniodes aristata*. This fern can tolerate a temperature of about 10–12°C (50–54°F), although its growth will be

slow as a result, and, like all other ferns, it still needs a high level of moisture to maintain healthy fronds.

Creating the same lush green effect as ferns in a cool, dry atmosphere can be done with *Fatsia japonica*, an evergreen shrub that actually prefers a winter resting temperature of about 7–10°C (45–50°F). Similarly, *Fatshedera lizei* (ivy tree) has small leaves and a fairly upright growth which can be trained into a more bushy and fern-like shape.

LEFT Pots of creamy miniature roses and pink trailing Pelargonium *(geranium) are combined with cerise spray carnations — a delightful arrangement for a summer lunch.*

BELOW LEFT Green recycled glass and ceramics contrast with lilac Exacum affine *(Persian violet) and* Campanula isophylla *(Italian bellflower).*

OPPOSITE For a dinner party, pale cream candles match the delicate flowers of three miniature roses.

F. benjamina by breeding varieties with small leaves, variegated leaves, oval and even crinkle-edged leaves.

BROMELIADS

In a modern dining room a decorative scheme could be based around a collection of houseplants from the bromeliad family, which includes *Ananas comosus*, an ornamental pineapple and the symbol of hospitality. Other close relations include *Aechmea fasciata* (urn plant), *Tillandsia lindenii*, *Guzmania lingulata* and *Vriesea splendens* (flaming sword). · Most of these plants have richly coloured, striped or banded leaves, dramatic bracts or flower spathes, and some also have exotic showy flowers which appear between spring and autumn and last for several weeks. As long as they have good bright, indirect light and reasonable humidity, bromeliads need little space in which to flourish. Grouped together on a low, angular table, they make a dramatic focal point and their exotic colours could be accentuated in other accessories in the room.

FRAGRANT FLOWERS

Filling a dining room with soft, natural perfume heightens the senses, particularly as a prelude to a delicious meal. In late winter and early spring small *Jasminum polyanthum* are available, often grown trained around a wire hoop. Just one plant will fill an entire room with its delicate perfume, which, like most white flowers, is at its most aromatic at night.

In smaller spaces where there is room merely for a dining table, chairs and perhaps one serving surface, a single, tall specimen plant may be the solution. *Ficus benjamina* (weeping fig) is a very graceful plant with masses of oval-shaped leaves which droop from arching branches. One large plant near a capacious and preferably full-length window adds elegance to both traditionally furnished rooms and simple modern interiors. Growers have responded to the great popularity of

Kitchens

ABOVE Look out for plants and containers that complement your china, table linen and glasses.

RIGHT Pots of basil or rocket add interest to summer salads, and just a few leaves give masses of flavour.

*E*very indoor gardener will want to include plants in the kitchen. Herbs on a windowsill are the obvious choice as the preparation and presentation of food are enhanced with the addition of a few freshly cut leaves, but there are also many fine decorative houseplants that will add interest to the kitchen area.

Finding a suitable location for plants in the kitchen is usually not a problem. There is often space either side of the kitchen window for some open shelving, a hanging shelf unit or a section of garden trellis from which plants can be tied or hooked. If the kitchen window is tall and narrow, it may be more practical to fix a shelf across it, 30 cm (12 in) or so from the top. Position it within easy reach if it is intended to house frequently used herbs. For decorative specimens, use the shelf as a platform for trailing plants. And if there is no available space for plants on any of the surfaces, then a hanging *étagère*, more often used for hanging pots and utensils, may be adapted to hold hanging or trailing plants.

Many kitchens also double up as dining areas, often divided by a peninsular unit or breakfast bar. An open shelf unit here suspended from the ceiling will help to screen the kitchen from the rest of the

OPPOSITE High shelves and hanging baskets provide permanent homes for lush green trailing plants without cluttering up kitchen surfaces.

LEFT Beaucarnea recurvata *and* Citrus mitis
are used to divide the space visually between a
kitchen and dining area, as well as providing
an attractive focal point.

THE KITCHEN GARDEN

Culinary herbs such as basil, borage, chervil, chives, sweet marjoram, mint, parsley, rosemary, sage, savory, tarragon and thyme will happily grow all year round on a sunny windowsill. With a large, well-lit site, it is also possible to grow tomatoes, aubergines (egg plants), peppers (capsicum), cucumbers and salad plants such as lamb's lettuce and rocket.

To maximize the range of your herb collection, it may be worth considering planting the harder and perennial varieties on an outside windowsill, provided, of course, that there is quick and easy access. Rosemary, savory, sage and thyme will grow in a well-drained window box as long as they are protected from wind and frost, freeing the inside sill for the more tender varieties.

Many supermarkets sell growing herbs in small plastic pots throughout the year, which are intended to be used immediately or within a week or so. For a quick, attractive display, place them straight into a more decorative planter and throw the herbs away as their leaves are depleted.

DECORATIVE PLANTS

A sunny windowsill is the ideal location for seasonal flowering plants and in particular spring bulbs such as *Galanthus*

room and provide another useful surface or two for plants.

One site for plants that should be avoided, however, is that annoying gap that some kitchen manufacturers leave between the top of the wall units and the ceiling. Unless the kitchen has skylights this is an impractical position as there is usually insufficient light for plants. In addition, the plants are difficult to reach to water and, being well above eye level, easily forgotten. Moreover, if trailing plants are displayed here, their tendrils tend to get caught in cupboard doors.

nivalis (snowdrop), *Hippeastrum* (amaryllis*)*, tulips and scented varieties such as narcissi and hyacinths. Depending on the temperature of the kitchen, the lifespan of these bulbs can be several weeks from the first signs of their shoots to the mature flowers and leaves. For perfect growth, they need full light; anything else will result in distorted stems and feeble flowers. However, a bowl of snowdrops grown with grass between the bulbs or a pot of fragrant hyacinths will not suffer if it is moved temporarily to provide a decorative centrepiece for the kitchen table.

Trailing specimens are good plants for a window shelf. *Rhoicissus rhomboidea* (grape ivy), *Asparagus plumosus* (asparagus fern), *Asparagus falcatus* and the *Columnea* family all like bright light but not full sun. These plants will provide a curtain of living green, negating the need for any

other window covering. The choice of varieties will depend on the ambient temperature of the kitchen – and none of them will appreciate a window leaking icy winter draughts. As most windows are located above the kitchen sink, this will give some degree of humidity. Nevertheless, to keep these plants in peak condition, mist them every day; keep a misting bottle next to the sink to jog your memory. For shelves – perhaps a unit that divides the kitchen from a

BELOW LEFT Many supermarkets sell herbs growing in small plastic pots which may be transplanted into more attractive containers. The herb pots can be discarded as the leaves are depleted for cooking.

BELOW RIGHT Flowering plants ring the changes throughout the year and can be chosen to coordinate with the kitchen's colour scheme.

dining area – compact, bushy plants rather than trailing species, are a good choice, including *Fittonia*, *Hypoestes*, *Peperomia caperata* and *Saxifraga stolonifera*. These plants like bright conditions, so, if there is only one window in the kitchen, remember to turn the plants regularly to ensure good, even growth.

Good hanging plants for a kitchen include ferns and vines, which provide lush greens, and the variegated leaves of *Scindapsus aureus*, *Philodendron scandens* (sweetheart plant) and tradescantia, all of which will introduce more colour into the room. Tradescantia is an ideal specimen for beginners. It grows rapidly in a bright, indirect light and has attractive green and white, or pink, green and white, leaves. Its fleshy stems do break off quite easily, but, if you gently press the broken stems into the soil, they will take root within a few days.

Bathrooms

RIGHT Mimosa
pudica *needs the*
high level of
humidity often
provided by
bathrooms. Its highly
sensitive leaves will
fold up tightly
if touched.

BELOW Covering the
topsoil of this
Dieffenbachia *with*
seashells adds a
decorative touch and
inhibits water loss.

The bathroom is often considered to be an environment ill-suited to houseplants for various reasons. Light levels in particular need to be considered as many bathrooms are quite dark, often with opaque glass at the window or semi-opaque curtains or blinds hung to ensure privacy. Some bathrooms, indeed, have no windows at all. High humidity and warmth are other considerations. However, some plants can thrive in the less extreme of these conditions and there are other solutions at hand to ensure that this room need not be neglected as a home for some very attractive plants.

TROPICAL DISPLAYS

The bathroom is the ideal location for most tropical plants where the warmth and humidity comes closest to their natural habitat, and there are a number which can also tolerate a low light level. These include *Aglaonema commutatum*, which has a decorative foliage of silver-green stripes, or almost painterly silver-green splashes, on large, spear-shaped leaves. *Maranta leuconeura* naturally grow under the protection of the leaf canopy in the tropical rainforests of South America. Their oval-shaped leaves are striped with

OPPOSITE Acorus
gramineus *is*
particularly suited
to cool and even
draughty rooms, and
needs a constantly
wet compost and
good humidity.

both white and shades of red and pink, introducing an element of colour into the room. *Maranta* rarely exceed about 20 cm (8 in) in height, but varieties of *Calathea*, a close relation, grow much larger. *Calathea makoyana* will reach a height of around 1 m (40 in). This is one of the easiest plants to grow in a bathroom with restricted light, and its oval leaves sport pretty markings: green spots on a cream-coloured background. Another popular variety is *Calathea zebrina*, which has long, arched leaves that are velvety in texture and are striped reddish purple. *Calathea*

BELOW Syngonium, Adiantum (maidenhair fern) and Nephrolepis exaltata bostoniensis are all ideal candidates for warm, well-lit and humid bathrooms.

crocata has deep green leaves and produces stunning saffron-yellow inflorescences on the ends of tall, erect stems.

A HOME FOR FERNS

Delicate ferns, such as *Microlepia strigosa*, *Pellaea rotundifolia*, and some varieties of *Adiantum* and *Pteris*, will survive indirect light as long as they are provided with warmth and humidity. A collection of these ferns would be particularly suited to a traditional style of bathroom, displayed in china and porcelain planters and cachepots. Frequent misting is essential to maintain healthy ferns, and this will also keep the delicate fronds and leaves free of any residue talcum powder or other toiletries sprayed in bathrooms.

A QUESTION OF SPACE

Where space is not a consideration, there are two ideal choices of specimen plants

ABOVE A wooden trug filled with a flowering Jasminum polyanthum *and* Rhododendron simsii *(azalea) is a short-term option in this windowless bathroom.*

for the bathroom. *Cyperus alternifolius* and *C. papyrus* are large, water-loving plants that actually like their roots permanently immersed in water – an excellent option for those who tend to overwater their plants. *Cyperus* need to be grown in a constantly wet medium with bright light conditions and a regular temperature of between 20–24°C (68–75°F) – the perfect bathroom atmosphere. In a modern bathroom a stylish way to house a *Cyperus* would be to stand it in a large aluminium waste bin or a huge glass planter filled with pebbles or water-retaining clay granules. *Monstera deliciosa* (Swiss cheese plant) is another large plant suited to the bathroom and an easy favourite, with glossy, dark green leaves perforated at the top of the plant to allow light to permeate down onto the lower branches. *Monstera* can grow up to around 2.5 m (7½ ft) and needs staking with a mossed stick to provide support for its numerous aerial roots.

If there are no free surfaces for plants, a decorative wire shelf unit or simple glass shelves supported with metal brackets could be fixed to a wall that receives the maximum amount of light. Another viable alternative for plants in a tiny bathroom, particularly one with roof lights, is to suspend them from the ceiling.

RIGHT A traditional-style bathroom is enhanced by a collection of plants housed in attractive china cachepots and wicker containers. Much-needed light is provided by a skylight.

Suitable plants for hanging containers include ivies, *Tolmiea menziesii* (piggyback plant) and *Scindapsus aureus*. These plants can also tolerate a slightly cooler temperature during the winter months, which may suit some bathrooms. Make sure that they are easy to reach for watering, either by lowering the pot or basket via a pully system or by using a watering can with an extra-long spout.

SHORT-TERM OPTIONS

Where natural light is very low or non-existent, keeping plants in a permanent position will be out of the question. In these cases, try to take a more flexible approach and move flowering plants into the room for the few weeks they are in bloom and take them back into better light conditions afterwards. Scented flowering plants are perfect for bathrooms: choose from *Jasminum polyanthum*, *Stephanotis floribunda*, hyacinth, *Convallaria majalis* (lily-of-the-valley) and *Gardenia jasminoides*, all of whose flowers are used in the production of perfume and are therefore particularly suitable for use in the bathroom.

Bedrooms

*N*o matter what the size of your bedroom, luxury and comfort are top priorities, and plants contribute to a sense of restful well-being. Surround yourself with healthy, attractive greenery and get rid of those plants that are past their best or on their last legs. Waking up to be greeted by a thriving group of plants is very therapeutic. Tiny rooms may only allow space for one or two small plants on the bedside table, whereas rooms on a grander scale offer scope for incorporating one of the large specimen palms or decorative fig trees. With the wide range of flowering plants now available right through the year, it is pleasing to co-ordinate both the colour and style of the flowers with the bedroom's decorative scheme. This is not a question of trying to match exactly plants with any floral fabric that may be in the room, but more a matter of taking any designs as a starting point, and a source of inspiration. By changing the plants every couple of months or so, you can keep the room looking new and fresh.

CLASSIC COLLECTION

A table positioned close to a window provides the surface for creating a

OPPOSITE Many bedrooms have little natural daylight so, rather than struggle to keep plants alive, use cut flowers, foliage or even silk alternatives. Some plants will, however, survive for several weeks with low light providing they are moved to a better-lit position to recover.

RIGHT This **Cattleya** *orchid adds exotic colour to a collection of personal and treasured objects. Kept cool, the flowers will last for several weeks. Let the surface dry out between waterings and remember that* **Cattleya***, like most orchids, prefer soft water.*

Left Pogonatheram paniceum *(house bamboo)*,
a large Nephrolepis exaltata bostoniensis *and*
a Chamaedorea elegans *(parlour palm) create*
a lush green and relaxing atmosphere.

tablescape, better known as a still life collection that groups together plants, objects and prized possessions on a table top. For instance, if you have a collection of seashells, driftwood and interesting pebbles on display, also add a couple of *Echeveria* to give the tablescape life. These desert succulents also grow in sand at the edge of a seashore. An assortment of richly coloured old china and glass would be complemented by the deep tones of *Saintpaulia* (African violet). These tiny rosette-shaped plants need to be kept slightly pot-bound to produce their distinctive purple, deep blue, pink or two-toned flowers. As *Saintpaulia* are best viewed from above, these make excellent tablescape plants.

Privacy is an important consideration in bedrooms, and, as an alternative to net or semi-opaque curtains, a table or *étagère* filled with plants and placed in front of a window provides a natural curtain for a room that is overlooked. Poor light will limit the choice of permanent plants elsewhere in the room, but disposable flowering varieties make a refreshing change and an alternative to cut flowers.

Just as a beautiful vase can make all the difference to the look and shape of a floral arrangement, so too can the choice of planter. Invest in something beautiful and in proportion to the plants you are most likely to buy. A soft blue ceramic pot could hold lilac hyacinths in spring, *Exacum* in summer, a contrasting yellow begonia in autumn and blue *Muscari* (grape hyacinth) to urge the end of winter.

For more permanent arrangements, *Pteris cretica* (ribbon fern) is a charming

bushy fern which can tolerate shade, but it does need a high level of humidity. Give a low bowl filled with several different varieties of *Pteris* seasonal colour by adding a single pot of primula, azalea, mini cyclamen or small varieties of summer bedding plants. As an alternative, you could create a pot-et-fleur, the expression used to describe a container display that includes both cut flowers and houseplants. One or more small vases placed between the pots of ferns could be filled with tiny blue *Myosotis* (forget-me-not) or clusters of white *Saponaria*. Even better would be an arrangement of fragrant flowers such as freesia, *Lathyrus odoratus* (sweet pea), *Acacia* or lavender. For the most pleasing effect, the flowers should look as though they are growing from between the plants, so avoid large-headed or tall blooms, which would look incongruous with delicate ferns. As the flower containers are concealed by the plants, you can use glass jars, plastic pots or even narrow vials pushed into the soil to hold single flower sprays.

Other shade-loving plants include all the members of the *Selaginella* family. *S. apoda* has thick, mossy foliage which appreciates being misted but hates strong light. There are also variegated relatives such as *S. martensii* as well as the creeper

S. kraussiana. These mosses need a humid atmosphere, so stand the pots on a layer of wet gravel in order to maintain the necessary level of moisture, or plant them in a terrarium or bottle garden. Terraria behave like mini greenhouses, and the modern versions often copy Victorian designs, making them delightful additions to period-style bedrooms.

BELOW A carefully pruned Sparmannia africana *(house lime) provides lots of gentle colour in this bedroom without taking up too much space.*

A plant more suitable for contemporary styles of furnishing is *Pogonatheram paniceum* (house bamboo), which is a grass related to the sugar-cane family. Its similarity to bamboo makes it a very pretty plant for bedrooms, and it has the same effect as an arching fern without being so

choosy about its living conditions. *P. paniceum* is happy situated in front of a sunny window along with a *Bambusa vulgaris* (common bamboo). Both these plants are relative newcomers to the houseplant world, and reflect the demand for soft-textured, delicate green foliage in our homes. They are both tropical plants, and will not tolerate cold or draughts.

Low temperatures also inhibit the intensity of perfumed plants such as gardenia and *Jasminum polyanthum*. Too large a plant or too many of them can produce a level of scent that is so overpowering it can make going to sleep difficult. Nevertheless, perfume is synonymous with bedrooms and other scented plants include *Stephanotis floribunda* and another new plant, bouvardia, which has very small clusters of white or pink flowers.

ABOVE The soft green foliage of Echeveria *and* Aechmea fasciata *(urn plant) enhance the atmosphere of a muted colour scheme, faded walls and washed floorboards.*

Halls and Corridors

The entrance hall is the first impression we gain of a home, and a blaze of living colour is a welcoming way to be greeted. Space for plants may be restricted to a hall table, but, if the hallway consists of a corridor that is too narrow even for this, then a small decorative shelf could offer an alternative venue for plants. You can visually enlarge the space by hanging a large mirror behind the table or shelf, which will also double the effect of any foliage and may help to reflect and amplify any available light on to the plants.

It is usually the lack of light which presents the biggest problem in hallways. Often the light source is distant and high up, forcing plants to devote all their energy to trying to reach it. You can overcome this restriction by treating all plants in the hallway as temporary visitors to be discarded and replaced as necessary. Another alternative is to rotate two or three plants. Aspidistra, for example, can tolerate a low level of light for short periods of time. Keep an identical plant elsewhere in the apartment and swap them over every two or three months. Aspidistra are also a good shape for a restricted space, as they are tall and narrow; those plants with a trailing or bushy growth will inevitably be continually brushed past and damaged. Many trailing plants can, however, be trained to grow more vertically. *Syngonium*, for example, has aerial roots that will cling to a mossed pole, which provides both support and essential moisture. Other plants that can be grown like this include *Philodendron scandens* (sweetheart plant), another vigorous climber, and *Schefflera arbicola*, which has leaves that resemble outstretched hands; the leaves are sometimes variegated with cream and yellow markings. The speed of growth will depend on the amount of light the plants receive, but one variety, *Schefflera actinophylla*, can thrive on very little.

Assuming, however, that the hall is bright, many climbing plants can be encouraged to grow up a trellis or up and around a hall mirror. *Rhoicissus capensis* is a fast-growing vine which can tolerate winter temperatures of as little as 5°C (41°F). So too can *Tetrastigma voinierianum*, a less well-known vine, which can grow 2–3 m (6–9 ft) in a year.

ABOVE Rhoicissus rhomboidea *(grape ivy),* Asparagus densiflorus *and* Scindapsus aureus *virtually fill this hall window.*

ABOVE Rhoicissus rhomboidea *(grape ivy) is an extremely popular plant as it will clamber up mossed poles, trellises or bannisters.*

LANDINGS AND STAIRWELLS

Landings and stairwells may support some living colour too. While the stairs themselves must always be kept free of obstacles, a corner shelf or tall pedestal placed at the turn of the stairs provides a safe platform for plants. A skylight offers the possibility of hanging plants. Easy-care varieties are the best choice for hanging plants as they can tolerate occasional neglect. Those plants with a constitution capable of surviving several weeks without water include *Rhoicissus rhomboidea* (grape ivy) and *Plectranthus australis*, both dark green ivies, and, for lighter and variegated foliage, numerous tradescantia and their close relative, *Zebrina pendula*, which, as its name suggests, is a perfect hanging plant. If the light source is abundant and directly overhead, it is worth making space for flowering climbing or trailing plants such as *Hoya bella*, a Burmese shrub with sweet-smelling clusters of white flowers that appear from spring to early autumn, and *Stephanotis floribunda*, which flowers at the same time. Some flowering plants such as *Passiflora* and *Jasminum* need a winter resting period in temperatures just below 10°C (50°F) if they are to flower again the following year; an unheated but light landing may provide just the conditions that are needed during the winter months.

A backdrop of lush foliage can always be supplemented in winter with seasonal flowering plants such as cyclamen, hyacinth and narcissi, which all prefer a cool atmosphere. It is very useful for the indoor gardener to have an area such as a landing to keep plants that are recovering from a spell in the dark or resting for the winter. If you keep flowering plants from one year to the next, group them together during the period when they are rather dull in a less prominent place in the apartment; they can then be moved into a prime position when they are about to bloom once again.

ABOVE Cocos weddeliana *(dwarf coconut palm) have very fine, narrow leaflets which complement the simplicity of this console table.*

Children's Rooms

Living in an apartment often inhibits children from having pets, and, while plants are not a substitute for a cat or dog, they do provide something to care for and watch growing. Indoor plants may only be a passing phase, as children grow out of hobbies extremely quickly, but any interest should be encouraged.

It is vital that any plants put in a child's room are not dangerous either through touch or ingestion. A small child will not register the difference between bright red berries which look like cherries or fleshy green leaves resembling juicy lettuce. Keep any hazardous plants out of the apartment or in positions where it is absolutely impossible for small hands to reach them.

GROW AND WATCH

Children like quick results, and visible growth is essential if you are to keep their attention. Hyacinth and narcissi bulbs planted in water-retaining clay granules or gravel will have exposed roots and green shoots after only a couple of weeks. Prepared bulbs are placed in glass containers filled with these granules or clean gravel so that their tops are just visible. Water is added until it is almost but not quite touching the bulbs. The

same form of hydroculture can also be used to grow plants such as *Scindapsus pictus*, *Zebrina pendula* or tradescantia.

Another way to introduce children to plants is to grow them from the pips of lemons, oranges and papayas, and the stones of lychees, mangosteens and avocados. A warm bright windowsill is the ideal spot for germinating these types of plants. Coffee beans and peanuts can also be germinated, provided they are both unroasted and unsalted!

ABOVE Growing hyacinth bulbs by hydroculture, either planted in gravel or suspended on a raft of sticks above water, will fascinate children.

Any plants that are easy to propagate will also appeal to children. *Saxifraga stolonifera* (mother of thousands), for instance, has long threadlike runners with mini plantlets at the ends which will immediately root when put into soil. Another member of the Saxifrage family, *Tolmiea menziesii* (piggyback plant), is more of a curiosity. The miniature plants develop at the base of its heart-shaped clusters of leaves and can be propagated straight away. Both these plants are best grown hanging from the ceiling or from a wall bracket, as is *Chlorophytum comosum* (spider plant), which is probably one of the most common and recognizable of the indoor plants.

PLANT COLLECTIONS

For a child who is developing collecting habits, a bottle garden or terrarium can mean a miniature fantasy jungle. Position this in front of a brightly lit window, and watch plants such as *Selaginella*, *Chamaedorea elegans*, *Kalanchoe* and the variegated leaves of *Fittonia* and *Hypoestes* thrive. Cacti are also popular with young plant collectors, but, as many of these plants have needle-like spikes, they should be selected carefully depending on the age and maturity of the child. Cacti can

be grown on a bright, sunny windowsill in a potting medium which resembles desert sand; commercially prepared soils are readily available. *Gymnocalycium*, *Notocactus*, *Mammillaria* and *Rebutia* are all easy cacti to grow and produce the most beautiful and brightly coloured flowers. Coming from the deserts of Central and South America, they can tolerate and thrive on a certain amount of neglect, provided they receive bright sun and are never overwatered.

Insect-eating plants hold a fascination for older children, and specimens such as

Dionaea muscipula (Venus fly trap), are very popular. This plant has succulent branches finishing in hinged and frilled leaf tips. When an insect lands on the pink inside tip, the leaf snaps shut and then slowly digests its victim. *Nepenthes* (pitcher plant) uses its scent glands to attract insects to its pitcher-shaped leaves and the slippery surface guides its unsuspecting visitor into the base of the leaf where it drowns in digestive juices. Procuring insects in winter may present a bit of a challenge, but this adds to the fun of keeping these plants.

Balconies, Patios and Window Boxes

*A*ny possibility of growing plants in an outside space is always greedily exploited by the enthusiastic indoor gardener – a passion for gardening can never be kept indoors if there is the slightest chance of growing plants in their natural element. The perfect dream for most plants and gardeners alike is the conservatory. In a conservatory plants receive light from all sides as they would in their natural habitat, the harmful effects of the sun can be alleviated by blinds, and there is total protection from wind, rain and frost. A patio or balcony does not offer the year-round possibilities of a conservatory, but, treated as a temporary garden (usually during the period from late spring to early autumn), it can provide several months of activity. Window boxes present the indoor gardener with many seasonal pleasures too, and a successful box will engage both your creativity and expertise.

BALCONIES AND PATIOS

Balconies, more than patios, can be very windy, especially on high buildings, and some form of wind-break is essential. Trellis screens can be both decorative and provide support for climbing plants. These may be permanent fixtures such as ivies, clematis or *Lonicera japonica* (Japanese honeysuckle), which has semi-evergreen leaves and sweet-smelling creamy flowers in summer. Unlike a proper garden, a seasonal space can largely be ignored for the rest of the year. Annual climbers such as *Lathyrus odoratus* (sweet pea) grow quite happily in pots and will reach up to

RIGHT On a small balcony, where space is at a premium, consider growing plants at different levels such as in waist-high window boxes or on shelves. Sheltered from the wind, frost and rain, many indoor plants may survive outdoors through the winter.

1–1.5 m (3–5 ft) during the season, producing a profusion of scented flowers that keep coming back after cutting. Runner beans not only provide a screen of lush green foliage but pretty red flowers, with the added bonus of a harvest of your own crop of home-grown vegetables.

Once the balcony is sheltered, it can then be considered a holiday residence for many houseplants that benefit from a spell outdoors, particularly *Chlorophytum*, *Fatsia*, hydrangea, jasmine and *Rhododendron simsii* (azalea). Many of the hardier tropical plants, such as yucca, *Schefflera*, *Cordyline* and *Coleus*, also like some warm fresh air. Available space will determine how many plants you have room for, but by investing in a multi-tiered *étagère* you can easily triple or quadruple the number of plants in one small area. Consider maximizing the wall space too by installing wall brackets from which to suspend hanging pots or to support a shelf or window box. Half-circular decorative containers or metal baskets are specially designed to fix directly to a wall. By utilizing vertical as well as horizontal space, you will not only leave room to sit and enjoy your temporary garden, but will also avoid putting too much weight on the balcony structure.

When it comes to containers, plastic pots and troughs may be inexpensive but they are hardly aesthetically pleasing; try "distressing" them with an oil-based paint to blend in with the greenery. Grow bags, while eminently practical, are exceedingly

LEFT With a rich compost and weekly feeding, tomatoes grow quite happily in tubs or pots along with other bedding plants, but need protection from the wind. Always include some scented varieties of flowers such as Lathyrus odoratus *(sweet pea).*

ugly to look at, so place them at the back of the balcony, and line up more decorative containers in front to conceal the bags themselves but not the growing contents. Reduce weight-loading problems by exchanging regular soil for light composts, which not only dry out more slowly but are richer and more concentrated in nutrients. Heavy containers are not a problem on patios, of course, but they may need to be frostproof.

Sharp, gusty winds can also be a problem at ground level. Whatever type of wind-break you consider, make sure that it does not obscure the light. Instead of going for a solid structure, it may be preferable to create a living wall of, say, eucalyptus trees or outdoor bamboo, both of which can be grown in large pots or tubs. If the patio is also semi-enclosed by a wooden or metal framework such as a pergola, any number of climbers can be grown up and around it to create a partial green ceiling which will protect the area below from the burning sun, heavy rain and the wind. This may not be desirable if your choice of plants includes sun lovers such as *Pelargonium* (geranium) or roses, however. Many patios are at a

semi-basement level and can be rather dark. Try painting the walls white, which will help to reflect sunlight and create a brighter atmosphere. A balcony or patio in semi-shade is still a fine summer residence for many houseplants, but you may also want to introduce some additional colour and texture. From late spring onwards a wide selection of bedding plants that can be grown in pots is available from nurseries and garden centres. Pansies, petunias, *Nemesia*, fuchsias and trailing varieties such as alyssum and lobelia are easy to maintain and will flower quite happily for three to four months.

WINDOW BOXES

Outdoor window boxes can be filled with both permanent and seasonal plants. Constant residents may include perennials such as *Lysimachia nummularia* (creeping jenny), *Arabis caucasiea*, *Aubretia deltoidea* (rock cress) and *Campanula* (bellflower).

ABOVE Outdoor window boxes filled with Pelargonium *(geranium) need to be brought indoors before the first frosts if they are to survive to the following year, unless the winter is particularly mild.*

All of these provide edging or trailing interest, although they may have to be cut back or divided every year or so to make room for the seasonal visitors; deep maroon heathers in winter, followed by hyacinths and crocuses for spring, with trailing lobelia and *Pelargonium* (geranium) throughout summer and autumn. Two or three varieties in profusion generally look better than one each of any number of randomly chosen plants.

The relationship of height between plants is also important, as a solid overall

ABOVE Hedera helix *(common ivy) can survive both indoors and outside, although plants will probably need more frequent watering if kept in a sunny position.*

shape makes more of an impact both from inside the window and as part of the building's exterior. Tall standard daffodils are often planted in commercial window boxes and more often than not end up horizontal, caught by gusts of spring wind. Dwarf tulips or fat-headed hyacinths are more resilient, especially if

they are protected by other, more bushy plants. As with all container gardening, window boxes may need considerable watering if they are packed with thirsty plants in a sunny position. Make sure that they can be reached safely and easily – and keep them planted throughout the year so that they are less likely to be forgotten. Wall-mounted boxes are usually permanently fixed, but a deep windowsill may safely hold a container that can be brought indoors to decorate the apartment for a special occasion.

Choosing plants for the right location

SUNNY WINDOWS

Allamanda cathartica

Aloe

Bambusa vulgaris

Beaucarnea recurvata

Bonsai

Bougainvillea

Cacti

Capsicum

Citrus mitis

Coleus

Echeveria

Euphorbia milii

Hibiscus

Hippeastrum

Kalanchoe

Pelargonium

Rosa

Solanum

Yucca

BRIGHT LIGHT

Acacia

Acalypha hispida

Achimenes hybrida

Aechmea fasciata

Araucaria heterophylla

Callistephus

Catharanthus roseus

Celosia

Chamaerops humilis

Codiaeum

Cycas revoluta

Dionaea muscipula

Euphorbia pulcherrima

Gerbera

Oxalis

Pachystachys

Passiflora caerulea

Tradescantia

LOW LIGHT

Aspidistra

Davallia

Hedera helix

Pellaea

Peperomia

Philodendron scandens

Pteris

Selaginella

HIGH HUMIDITY

Abutilon

Adiantum

Caladium

Gerbera

Cattleya

Cyperus

Dionaea muscipula

Gardenia

Miltonia

Nephrolepis

Phalaenopsis

DRY ATMOSPHERE

Aloe

Beaucarnea recurvata

Bougainvillea

Cacti

Dracaena

Eustoma grandiflorum

Hibiscus

Kalanchoe

Phoenix canariensis

Yucca

Zebrina

Euphorbia milii

WARM CONDITIONS

Allamanda cathartica

Anthurium

Aphelandra

Begonia

Caladium

Crossandra

Nephrolepis

Passiflora caerulea

COOL CONDITIONS

Aspidistra

Crocus

Cyclamen persicum

Eucalpytus

Hedera helix

Hyacinthus

Muscari

Narcissus

Pelargonium

Tulips

Sansevieria trifasciata

POTENTIALLY HARMFUL PLANTS

Arum – toxic if eaten/skin and eye irritant

Browallia – harmful if eaten

Datura – toxic if eaten

Dieffenbachia – toxic if eaten/skin and eye irritant

Dipladenia sanderi – harmful if eaten

Euonymus – harmful if eaten

Euphorbia – harmful if eaten/skin and eye irritant (except new *Euphorbia pulcherrima* hybrids)

Gloriosa – toxic if eaten

Primula obconica

Hedera – harmful if eaten/may cause a skin allergy

Hyacinthus – skin irritant

Ipomoea – harmful if eaten

Iris – harmful if eaten

Narcissus – harmful if eaten/skin irritant

Nerium oleander – toxic if eaten

Primula obconica – may cause skin allergy

Schefflera – may cause skin allergy

Scilla – harmful if eaten

Solanum – toxic if eaten

Tulipa – skin irritant

SHORT-TERM PLANTS

Begonia elatior

Browallia

Calceolaria herbeohybrida

Callistephus

Capsicum annuum

Celosia cristata

Chrysanthemum indicum

Crocus

Cyclamen

Dahlia

Dianthus

Euphorbia pulcherrima

Eustoma grandiflorum

Gerbera jamesonii

Impatiens

Lilium

Mimosa pudica

Muscari

Narcissus

Osteospermum

Primula

Schizanthus retusus

Senecio cruentus

Torenia fournieri

PLANTS FOR BOTTLE GARDENS AND TERRARIA

Acorus gramineus

Begonia rex

Calathea

Dionaea muscipula

Ferns

Fittonia

Hedera helix

Hypoestes

Orchids, miniature (terraria only)

Peperomia caperata

Pilea

Saintpaulia (terraria only)

Selaginella

THE SEASONAL INDOOR GARDEN

Each season brings a fresh array of flowers and plants to add natural colour to your apartment. Planning for each season can provide varied arrangements of colour and shape both for inside the home and for balconies, patios and window boxes.

Spring

BELOW Once these bulbs have finished flowering they can be planted out and naturalized in a garden where they will flower the following spring.

*W*ith the warmer weather and brighter light of spring comes the desire for more activity around the home. Just as outdoor gardens are bursting with life, so too are houseplants, and this is the time of year when they need increased watering and regular feeding. It is an ideal time to reassess the indoor garden, checking each plant for any signs of disease or pests as well as the need for possible repotting.

Reassessing your plant collection may require some ruthless decisions, and some plants may well be past their sell-by date and need throwing away. Re-creating ideal growing conditions is often difficult, and after two or three years *Dracaena* and some palms and ferns can look decidedly leafless and unattractive. Regrouping or repositioning plants gives a new look to an interior, but, as most plants hate being moved, make sure that the new conditions exactly replicate the previous site as well as being aesthetically pleasing. Buying one or two new plants to add to an existing group is another solution, and spring offers a wide choice of flowering plants. Growth habit is worth considering when buying new plants to replace those that have not survived the winter or are past their prime. It is easy to be seduced by the new array of plants displayed in garden centres and to forget to take into account how much they will grow.

SPRING BULBS

Early in the year pots of bulbs brighten up windowsills and add colour to well-lit spots. Narcissi, crocuses, hyacinths and *Galanthus* (snowdrops) will last for several weeks if they are kept cool. Bulbs planted outside in pots from previous years can

OPPOSITE Terracotta pots filled with spring flowers – Iris recticulata, crocuses and primulas – will brighten up the smallest patio, balcony or entrance. The pots would also flourish inside for a few weeks if kept somewhere light and cool.

flower indoors will do so only once; after flowering, they must be planted outside if they are to bloom again. Several lilies grown together and presented in a mossed basket make a dramatic centre-piece in a room, and if kept cool will last for several weeks. Snip off faded blooms to encourage the other buds to open. The trumpet-shaped *Lilium longiflorum* (Easter lily), has very fragrant flowers, and so has *L. regale* and the variety *L. regale* 'Mount Everest'. Bowl-shaped lilies such as *L. auratum* and *L. speciosum* (Japanese lily) have flared petals, often with dramatic stripes and speckles. The less-expensive, mid-century hybrids have wonderful, brightly coloured flowers – red, orange and yellow, crimson and gold – but are unperfumed.

BELOW Muscari armeniacum *(grape hyacinth),* Scilla siberica *(Siberian squill) and hyacinths may all be planted in autumn at varying intervals to give a constant display throughout late winter and the spring.*

ABOVE For a colourful spring arrangement, potted tulips can be quickly transplanted into a basket lined with plastic; cover the topsoil with a layer of moss.

be brought inside as they are about to flower, as long as the bulbs are gently acclimatized to the change in tempera-ture. *Scilla sibirica* (Siberian squill) and *Muscari* (grape hyacinth) will grow in the same pot for several years, although their flowering time may vary from year to year depending on the weather.

As the season progresses and the early spring bulbs fade, put them back outside or give them away to people with gar-dens where they can be planted out and naturalized. Supplement their colour indoors with lilies newly bought in bud or previously planted in autumn through to late winter. Like other bulbs, lilies that have been specially prepared to

SPRING SHRUBS

There are a number of shrubs that have a magnificent spring display and will survive indoors. Camellia were once considered to be suitable only for warm greenhouses or heated conservatories, but the new hybrids will happily thrive in a container placed on a sheltered patio or balcony. Bring them indoors as they start to flower in early to mid-spring; if kept in cool conditions, the full beauty of their exotic flowers can be enjoyed for a month or so. If you are buying new plants such as camellia, always purchase them in flower or with coloured buds, partly so you can see what the flowers look like, and also to make sure that the plants will actually come into bloom.

An evergreen shrub also available in spring is *Cytisus canariensis* (genista), a plant familiar to those who have taken a spring holiday on the Canary Islands. Between late winter and mid-spring, *Cytisus* produce brilliant yellow racemes of flowers, which are slightly scented, on arching branches. These plants can grow to about 1 m (3 ft) in height and need an outdoor spot in summer.

COLOURFUL AND SCENTED PLANTS

Fragrant spring plants other than scented bulbs include *Stephanotis floribunda*, which appear in late spring, and *jasminum polyanthum*, which come into flower earlier in the year. Both these species need constant warm and humid conditions in order to flower again the following year. *Citrus mitis*

is less demanding. Originating from the Philippines, this miniature orange tree has dark green glossy leaves and tiny scented flowers in late spring. These develop into decorative fruits which are edible but taste extremely bitter. Leave them on the plant unless you want to make marmalade with them. *C. mitis* appreciates a bright and sunny position and enjoys a summer holiday outdoors,

ABOVE Spring-flowering Galanthus nivalis *(snowdrops) and crocuses – all white, with a dash of yellow – have been grown in a collection of old white-glazed china containers.*

which aids pollination of the flowers; it also prefers cool conditions in the winter. Although it is considered to be a dwarf variety, *C. mitis* can in fact grow to over 1 m (3 ft) in height.

Another plant which offers the same glossy green and orange colouring as *Citrus mitis* is *Clivia miniata* (kaffir lily), a subtropical rhizome which produces a single stem with a cluster of bright orange, lily-shaped flowers in early spring. This plant, like the members of the orchid family, loves being pot-bound and often reaches a height of 45–65 cm (18–26 in) in a 14-cm (5½-in) pot.

Schizanthus retusus is an annual that has been recently cultivated as a houseplant too. It has fern-like foliage and masses of butterfly-shaped flowers with speckled yellow centres and outer petals that come in a range of colours from cerise to pale pink, deep red and purple. *S. retusus* needs bright light and is ideal for indoor or outdoor window boxes. *Senecio cruentus* hybrids are also good candidates for indoor or outdoor window boxes. Available in every colour except yellow, these daisy-shaped flower clusters last for two months and, unlike *Schizanthus*, can tolerate a cooler temperature, so a north-facing window (south-facing in the Southern hemisphere) is perfect.

TROPICAL PLANTS

Many tropical plants are cultivated to flower in spring; these include *Anthurium* with its bright red or white spathes; *Spathiphyllum*, which has tall, white spathes, and the numerous exotic bromeliads. These plants need to be assessed for their long-term appeal with or without flowers, as they may not flower again after the

ABOVE The brightly-coloured faces of two auriculas are seen in sharp relief against the dark paint of a corner shelf.

first season. One of the more reliable flowering sub-tropicals is *Pachystachys lutea* from Brazil and Peru, which starts to bloom in early spring. This evergreen plant has long, dark green leaves and produces between seven and eight stems with 15 cm (6 in) flower spikes. These bright yellow, lolly-shaped bracts last for three or four months and the actual flowers, which are about 5 cm (2 in) long and pure white, appear after a month or so but fade after a few days.

HERBS

As well as being decorative, many plants bought or grown in spring can also have a practical application. Herbs need to be sown or bought as seedlings in spring if they are to reach maturity by summer. Perennials such as bay, chives, marjoram, sage and mint may need repotting in spring, and rosemary, which produces pretty pale lilac flowers early in the year, is a welcome addition to any kitchen windowsill. Annual herbs such as chervil, basil and parsley, for example, can be grown from seed, but, if only a couple of pots are required, it is less time consuming and more economical to buy seedlings from a garden centre. Parsley, one of the most popular herbs, is notoriously difficult to germinate.

A window box is the ideal site for growing herbs. Imagine one filled with the white flowers of thyme, marjoram and savory, and given contrast by adding the lilac globe flowers of chives and the bright purple flowers of borage. Generally, herbs need lots of sunshine and a light, fertile and well-drained soil. Keeping them in pots contains their growth habit; this is particularly important with mint, which can easily take over a window box, strangling all the other inhabitants. If the herbs are kept in individual pots, they can be grouped together attractively in a window box, enabling annuals or exhausted varieties to be easily removed during the year without disrupting the others. Both lavender and rosemary have very aromatic leaves and, if placed in low pots near the entrance to a patio or balcony, their sweet fragrance is released as people brush past them.

Creating a springtime basket

A wooden trug filled with a variety of spring bulbs and plants makes an attractive alternative to a vase of seasonal flowers. It provides a delightful centrepiece for a dining table or could be given as an original Easter present. A seed tray would make a less-expensive option, as would a shallow wooden crate. A wide variety of seasonal plants may be used, but avoid very tall daffodils or tulips which may topple over in a shallow container. Primula, *Muscari armeniacum* (grape hyacinth), *Scilla sibirica* (Siberian squill), crocuses, *Galanthus nivalis* (snowdrops) and miniature irises are all available at this time of year.

1 Line the trug or box with a piece of thick plastic and cover this with a layer of broken crocks. These will help to keep the plastic in place and will also provide drainage.

2 Miniature narcissi, primula, **Muscari armeniacum** (grape hyacinth) and a couple of variegated ivies are arranged together with a thick layer of moss to fill any gaps.

ABOVE Kept in a light position that is consistently cool, this arrangement should last for several weeks. As individual plants fade they can easily be replaced with others.

Summer

Summer is the season when the atmospheric conditions outside and inside come closest together and many houseplants can become outdoor plants for a couple of months. Most tropical and subtropical plants respond to a spell out-doors, although they cannot tolerate full sun. In their native habitats they grow beneath a canopy of leaves which pro-vides an effective filter to sunlight. Neither can many of these plants cope with strong winds or cold rain, as they often have soft, fleshy stems or brittle branches that are easily damaged in adverse weather conditions. Tropical and subtropical plants can survive inside all year round, but increasing the amount of light that they receive and raising the humidity levels will encourage them to grow and, in some cases, to flower.

SUMMER FLOWERS

Of interest to the kitchen windowsill are the scented-leaf varieties of *Pelargonium* (geranium) that release a fragrance of apple, lemon, peppermint or nutmeg when the leaves are rubbed or crushed between the fingers. These aromatic leaves can be used to flavour sweets, cakes and puddings, and their bushy foliage and pink or white flowers are a very pretty addition to any sunny windowsill, inside or outside. The flowers are generally quite insignificant, however, compared to those of *P. grandiflorum* (regal geranium), which have large, azalea-shaped flowers. *P. grandiflorum* will flower from spring to autumn and need pinching back to keep their bushy shapes in order. *P. zonale* (zonal geranium), which are popular outdoor bedding plants, are best treated as annuals unless they can be moved to a greenhouse or conservatory for the winter months. Stem cuttings are easy to take; prepare these in summer and over-winter in a cool, bright place for the following year.

Ivy-leaf varieties of geranium that are popular for outdoor hanging baskets may

BELOW Begonia elatior *is grown for its flowers which form a dense mass of double or single heads in every colour range except blue. Normally discarded after flowering, it can be kept going for the following year.*

OPPOSITE While Yucca elephantipes *(spineless yucca) can tolerate direct light,* Dracaena marginata *and the white-flowered* Spathiphyllum wallisii *may need protection from the hottest summer sun.*

also be trained along a trellis, around a window frame or left to cascade from wall-hung pots. To promote continuous flowering, keep them pot-bound, make sure they get lots of bright sunshine, and dead head them regularly. Given the same conditions, *Thunbergia alata* and the trailing varieties of *Tropaeolum majus* (nasturtium) are easily trained to grow up a trellis or similar support.

Many bedding plants are being bred for indoors and one of the most popular is *Impatiens hawkeri*. This hybrid, which is derived from a plant native to tropical New Guinea, is now being cultivated to produce every shade of red and pink flowers. It has bright green, fleshy foliage and vibrantly coloured flowers. Try combining it with the similarly bushy but larger *Begonia elatior*. Group together harmonizing colours of peach and pink, scarlet, cerise and bright orange, or pale cream and lemon to blend with an interior scheme or to complement china and table linen for informal summer lunches and dinner parties.

Dwarf varieties of *Dahlia variablis* and *Zinnia elegans* grown in pots on a sunny outside windowsill can be quickly transferred into a large container for an indoor display where they will thrive quite happily for several days. Blue flowers are synonymous with summer gardens and for indoors there is a small variety of plants including *Brunfelsia*, *Browallia*, *Campanula isophylla* (Italian bellflower) and the more recent and delightful *Eustoma*

grandiflorum which also produce white flowers. Until quite recently, *E. grandiflorum* was available only as a cut flower, known as *Lisianthus russelianus*. Using growth inhibitors, it is now bred as an indoor plant reaching 40–60 cm (16–24 in) in height and producing large, papery flowers in varying shades of purple, pink or cream.

Other varieties being cultivated as indoor plants and intended to last for one season are *Torenia fournieri*, *Gerbera jamesonii* and *Schizanthus retusus*. Some varieties can be encouraged to last for up to two or even three years before they become too straggly and these include *Osteospermum*, *Rosa chinensis* and *Argyranthemum frutescens* (marguerite). All

ABOVE Pelargonium *(geranium) are best treated as annuals unless they can be moved to a greenhouse or conservatory during the winter.*

these plants demand bright light and plenty of space in order to maintain their flowers throughout the season; the area close to windows may be at a premium.

SUMMER FRUITS

Outdoor gardeners with a small garden are often faced with the decision of how much space to devote to flowers and how much to edible plants. For the indoor gardener with only windowsills to work with, practical decisions need to be made. A large, sunny window suits some fruits such as *Lycopersicon esclentum* (tomato), *Cucumis sativus* (cucumber) and *Solanum melongena ovigerum* (aubergine/egg plant). Apart from *Fortunella margarita* (kumquat) and *Fragaria vesca sempervirens* (strawberry), any other fruit is not worth attempting indoors without a conservatory. Select dwarf varieties of tomato, water them daily and feed twice a week. Hybrid-cucumber plants grow to between 1–1.5 m (40–57 in), and a row of pots will fill a sunny window. Try interspersing these with *Capsicum grossum* (sweet pepper), which grow to a similar height. These create a green curtain that could also act as a filter to protect more light-vulnerable plants placed just beyond the window.

All these plants are prone to insect infestation and need constant monitoring, misting and watering. Less demanding is *Hibiscus esculentus* (okra), which produces a 1-m (3-ft) high vine-like plant with pretty yellow flowers followed by green

pods. The pods are used for thickening soups and stews, and are found in West African and Jamaican curries.

Summer meals invariably include salads, and a handful of fresh herbs adds visual interest and relish to spinach and lettuce greens, which can also be raised if they are planted out in grow bags on a balcony or patio. They are less successful grown indoors, and even on a windowsill lettuce tends to grow rather leggy. As each plant takes two or three months to develop, it seems rather a lot of effort

ABOVE Many flowers are edible, including borage, chives, roses and pansies, and the bright orange Tropaeolum majus *(nasturtium) adds a peppery flavour to salads.*

for little return. *Tropaeolum majus* (nasturtium) produce a succession of bright orange flowers that add colour and a peppery flavour to salad greens all summer long. Other edible flowers include borage, chives, roses and pansies. Snip off the flower heads just before they are needed and be careful not to use flowers

that have been recently sprayed with pesticides or fungicides. Ideally, any plant that needs spraying with chemicals should be placed in a well-ventilated room away from furnishings, children and pets. Keep sick plants isolated until you are sure that the infection or pests have been completely eradicated. One side-effect of using chemicals is that the plants may lose all their flowers, but with good care, watering and feeding these should start to form again once the plants have fully recovered from the treatment.

*LEFT This spread of summer colour includes
(from left to right):* Osteospermum,
Campanula isophylla *(Italian bellflower),*
Zantedeschia aethiopica, *hibiscus and begonia.*

population. Systemic fungicides and modern systemic pesticides are safe and effective, and neither pests nor diseases generally prove fatal if treated quickly.

SUMMER BREAKS

Care and attention are, of course, the best preventions against pests and diseases, but providing these can present a dilemma for the indoor gardener who is about to go away on a summer holiday. By far the most effective solution is a plant-sitter, preferably someone who is prepared to stay in the house full time or a regular visitor who can maintain the watering and feeding routine. You can

AVOIDING PESTS AND DISEASES

Improving the air circulation with lots of open windows is good for plants and humans, but this also raises the risk of insect invasion. Apartments are generally less prone to this problem than are houses with gardens, but a patio or balcony and even a window box may attract unwelcome visitors such as whitefly, greenfly and thrips. Most insects can be successfully eradicated before too much harm is done, but their minute size often means they go undetected until the damage becomes noticeable. Once the infestation is serious, the plant may never recover, but it should be treated immediately anyway and isolated from other plants. Constant inspection negates drastic measures, and, as watering is likely to be a weekly or twice-weekly event during

the summer, this should become the time for a regular bug check too. Many insects prefer to live on the undersides of leaves, so these also need to be inspected diligently.

Keeping the windows shut is not a practical solution to controlling insects, and the resulting stuffiness and poor air circulation is the perfect atmosphere for plant diseases to flourish. Common infections such as mildew, sooty mould and botrytis are generally due to overwatering, insufficient drainage and poor ventilation, all problems that are more likely to occur in winter than in summer. However, as summer is the most popular time for holidays, permanently shut windows, an unseasonably cool fortnight and a neighbour prone to overwatering may allow a disease to spread through the plant

*ABOVE The complementary colours of a
miniature rose,* Kalanchoe manginii, *hibiscus,*
Coleus blumei, *gerbera, begonia and*
Mimulus *provide a vivid display.*

help by placing plants together, which increases humidity, and by grouping them by watering requirements. Standing plants on trays covered with a layer of wet stones or gravel also increases humidity; top up the trays with water regularly. Leave a clear note next to each plant or group of plants specifying how much and how often they need watering.

Outside plants, provided they are out of direct sunlight, can generally stand a few days without watering, but if they are flowering and growing any longer may be disastrous. Cover the pot surface with a thick mulch of chipped bark or moss to help retain the moisture in the soil and to keep the roots cool. An automatic watering system is another option for patio or balcony plants, although it is expensive and looks unattractive unless all the pipework can be concealed in some way. The system consists of a network of pipes connected to a timer which activates the system at given daily or weekly intervals. The water is served via thin hoses punctuated with tiny holes that have been inserted at intervals along the pipes. This system is not practical for indoor use and most of the various irrigation devices for indoor plants are designed for one pot only, which means that the cost can add up. It would be better to spend the money on a present to thank a well-briefed and willing neighbour.

If you are going on holiday, try not to buy new plants or to germinate seeds just before you go. If this is unavoidable, give

LEFT A bowl of Clerodendrum thomsoniae *will need to be pruned regularly to encourage flowering. Modern hybrids are treated with growth inhibitors as the original shrub can grow up to 4 m (13 ft).*

the new plants a neutral position – that is, in reasonable, indirect light. Cover a tray of tiny seedlings with clear film (plastic wrap) or place the tray in a plastic bag and secure the opening. Moisture will condense on the plastic and drip back on to the soil. This method is a short-term solution, as seedlings can grow by 2–3 cm (¾–1¼ in) in just a few days. Remember to leave space above the soil to allow the seedlings to develop.

New growth and flowering plants need feeding as well as watering in the summer

months, and most houseplants respond to a diluted liquid fertilizer once a week. Combining feeding with watering is the easiest method, and it is also an effective way of keeping plants topped up with vital minerals. Some plants prefer to be underfed and respond by producing a greater profusion of flowers. *Pelargonium* (geranium) reward the gardener with lots of healthy foliage if fed regularly, but keep them in a less fertile and more arid soil, and they will produce continuous flowers throughout the season.

Creating a *pot-et-fleur*

Pot-et-fleur is literally French for "pot and flower", and is an expression used to describe an arrangement of cut flowers with houseplants. In summer, when both flowering plants and cut flowers are in abundance and relatively cheap, you can afford to be a little more extravagant with the size of your displays. Trailing plants offer more versatility as fewer plants are needed to fill a container and their long branches may be intertwined between the cut flowers, both filling any gaps and offering a natural means of support. As well as training *Pelargonium* (geranium), you could also use *Hedera helix* (common ivy), *Scindapsus aureus*, the flowering *Thunbergia alata* (black-eyed Susan) or *Campanula isophylla* (Italian bellflower).

1 You will need a large terracotta or ceramic container with a flat bottom, a piece of tough plastic, pots or jam jars (two-thirds the height of the container), five pots of trailing Pelargonium (geranium) and a selection of summer flowers.

2 Line the container with plastic. Fill with jam jars or pots and wedge them securely. Half-fill the jars with water.

3 Position the Pelargonium (geranium) pots to form a circle around the edge, resting each pot on the jam jar or pot below.

4 Place the flowers in the jars, making sure they go into the water and not into any spaces in between.

OPPOSITE To create a bright Mediterranean pot-et-fleur use Helianthus annus (sunflower), brilliant blue delphiniums and deep cerise Dianthus (spray carnation). The flowers should last at least a week.

Autumn

BELOW Pachystachys lutea *comes from Peru and is often confused with* Beloperone guttata. Pachystachys *has bright yellow bracts which last several months, while the tiny white flowers which emerge from them last only a few days.*

*M*any flowering plants bought or grown in the summer will continue to bloom well into the autumn if they are carefully watered and fed regularly. *Streptocarpus*, bouvardia, *Saintpaulia* (African violet), *Pelargonium* (geranium) and fuchsia are all plants capable of producing flowers until mid-autumn and beyond. Other, more seasonal varieties can also be introduced at thie time: flame-coloured chrysanthemums, *Callistephus* and autumn bulbs all bring welcome colour into the home.

As the days get shorter and there is a noticeable chill in the air, bring in any plants that have been holidaying on a balcony or patio. An early frost is just as likely as a late heatwave, and valuable and prized plants can be lost overnight. As you return them to their winter habitat, check each one meticulously for any signs of disease or insect infestation. Insects multiply rapidly indoors and quickly spread to other juicy-looking victims. Remove any dead leaves or straggly branches and give each plant a general tidy up before giving it house room.

SEASONAL OFFERINGS

To mark the change in season, introduce varieties that are closely associated with autumn. Although chrysanthemums are now widely available all year round, those with rich, red, auburn and bronze flowers reflect the colour of trees and shrubs outdoors as they turn. The variety most commonly available is *Chrysanthemum indicum*, which is a small, bushy plant that stands between 24–30 cm (9½–12 in) high. Care is needed when buying these plants, as the temptation is to select those with tight green buds in order to obtain the longest flowering life. In fact, these plants are too immature and

OPPOSITE As a cut flower, Eustoma grandiflorum *can stand well over 1 m (3 ft) high but, using growth inhibitors, plant breeders are producing small plants suitable for table arrangements.*

may never flower, so it is advisable to choose those with lots of good-coloured buds. Given cool conditions, they will flower for between six and eight weeks and further buds will be encouraged to open if you snip off faded blooms. Another variety, *C. morifolium*, is best regarded as a disposable plant; after its term in the house it can be planted in a friend's garden, where it will flower again but in a taller and less bushy form.

Callistephus hybrids are being bred for autumn pot plants and resemble chrysanthemum flowers, although the leaves are less frond-like. More commonly known as a bedding plant, special cultivation and growth inhibitors have produced a small, bushy shape capable of producing a mass of flowers for six to eight weeks. Unlike chrysanthemums, they can tolerate a hotter, sunnier position. Available in autumnal shades, there are also some extremely pretty pink and lilac varieties. Dead head the plants regularly and throw away after flowering.

Another easy and disposable plant is *Capsicum annuum* (ornamental chilli pepper, Christmas pepper), which has small, star-shaped white flowers. In a bright, sunny position these develop into green peppers that gradually ripen into purple, crimson or orange and yellow edible fruits, lasting for up to about three months. Without some

direct sun the peppers will not mature properly, and if kept in dim light the fruits will just drop off; it is possible, however, to buy *C. annuum* when it is already at the fruiting stage.

It is important not to confuse *C. annuum* with the very similar-looking but poisonous *Solanum pseudocapsicum*. This cheerful-looking plant has larger, round berries that resemble red cherry tomatoes, and the leaves are shorter. It is available in late autumn and the berries can last for several months. Unlike the true *C. annuum*, it is a perennial and needs a period outdoors in summer if it is to bear fruits again the following year.

All the plants mentioned so far are short and bushy. Grouped together in

BELOW Kalanchoe manginii *and* Hibiscus rosa-sinensis *produce flowers in similar autumnal tones, and are ideally suited as they both prefer direct light and a warm environment.*

low containers on a dining or hall table, they mark the onset of a change in season and last so much longer than a bunch of autumn cut flowers. A larger arrangement could be made by placing a vase of autumnal leaves such as copper beech behind a group of orange and red pepper plants. Ornamental gourds are also around at this time and, lighly varnished, add another dimension to a tablescape.

For a completely different style of flowering plant, cymbidium orchids are becoming very popular as easy indoor plants. Modern hybrids are very different from those that the Victorians took such great pains to grow in specialized conservatories and greenhouses, although they still like warmth, humidity and indirect light. The rhizomes or tuberous roots of the plant prefer to be kept pot-bound, so a very small planter will accommodate an orchid about 1 m (3 ft) tall. The arching stem, which carries a spray of up to 30 flowers, is usually supported by a stake as it is inevitably top heavy. Choose plants with the lowest flowers open and lots of healthy-looking coloured buds and these will open and last from between eight to ten weeks. After flowering, the plant needs resting, preferably in a greenhouse or conservatory.

More difficult to maintain but with the advantage that it flowers virtually throughout

ABOVE Mirrors can be used to great effect with plants, creating a lavish double image and increasing light levels. Cattleya orchids may need a stick to support the heavy flower stalk.

the year is *Phalaenopsis* (moth orchid). It needs a constant and humid temperature of 16°C (60°F) in winter and 25°C (76°F) in summer and autumn, and between ten and 15 hours of light each day, which means providing an artificial light source in winter. This should not put off the indoor gardener, as with sufficient warmth and humidity the plant will remain in flower for about three to four weeks. It then should be discarded or passed on to someone with a greenhouse or conservatory. It requires a tiny pot and has six or

seven leaves at compost level with one tall stem supporting exceptionally beautiful flowers in shades of pink or white. A single plant creates a stunning focal point in a cool living room or bedroom.

For dramatic impact, *Aphelandra squarrosa* is worth looking for in autumn. It is known as the zebra plant because of its

creamy white veins on large, oval-shaped, dark green glossy leaves. It is also called saffron spike because in autumn it produces bright yellow bracts from which rather insignificant white flowers appear. Originating from tropical South America, this plant is considered difficult, but this is only because it demands a very humid atmosphere. The plant should be bought in flower as these bracts last from between four to six weeks, after which the plant still remains an attractive specimen. When the bracts have faded, they should be snipped off and the plant can then be moved to a cooler temperature of around 12°C (54°F), but, like all tropical plants, it cannot stand extreme cold or draughts. It prefers warm, soft water and it should be fed once a week in spring until the bracts appear, when it will need a double dose each week.

BULBS

As so many plants are available throughout the year it is worth finding some that do still respect the seasons, and bulbs are one such group. *Colchicum autumnale* is a bulb sold in mid- and late-summer for autumn flowering. Commonly called the autumn crocus, it is no relation to the spring flower that it resembles. Specially prepared bulbs can be grown in the same pot for a period of up to four years and require a constant temperature of about 18°C (65°F).

Autumn planting of spring bulbs needs careful planning to ensure a continual succession of flowers through the final months of the year and into spring. Spacing out your planting at two- to three-week intervals ensures a constant and varied display. A wide variety of bulbs is specially prepared for indoor cultivation and the easiest to grow are hyacinths, with tulips probably being the most difficult. Always choose bulbs as you would onions: good-sized and firm with a clean, unblemished skin. Bulb fibre is easily obtainable to line the base of a bowl. Place the bulbs on top, close

ABOVE Gerbera jamesonii *is a perennial plant, now being bred as an indoor houseplant available all year round.*

together but not touching either the sides of the bowl or each other. Fill with compost until just the tips of the bulbs are showing. Cover completely with a black plastic bag or put the bowl in a cupboard out of the light and ensure that the temperature never rises above 7°C (45°F). This is known as the plunging period when the root system starts to develop. Any light at this stage will inhibit healthy growth but check from time to time to ensure that the compost is still moist.

After six to ten weeks or when the shoots are about 2.5–4 cm (1–1¾ in) high, move to a shady spot and then after a couple of days to a bright position to flower. A temperature not exceeding 21°C (70°F) is ideal and the bowl needs

to be turned to allow regular growth. After flowering, the blooms but not the stalks should be removed, and watering continued until the leaves wither. If you have a garden, remove the bulbs and keep them cool and dry so that they can be planted out the following autumn. If you don't have a garden, throw or give them away. Another option is to grow *Narcissus* 'Paperwhite' and hyacinths in clay water-retaining pebbles contained in a glass pot so that the roots are visible. Keep the water level just below the bottoms of the bulbs.

Other bulbs sold in autumn are the *Hippeastrum* hybrids (amaryllis), which, unlike narcissi, tulips and crocuses, are truly indoor bulbs and cannot tolerate growing outdoors. *Hippeastrum* have one fat stem which grows before the leaves and can be between 70–90 cm (28 in–3 ft) tall. It produces a crown or three or four huge lily-like flowers. After they have faded, the bulb is left in the pot until the foliage has died down and the plant is then rested until growth starts again, usually about a year later. Finding space to accommodate these bulbs may present a problem as they are rather unattractive when resting.

If you have a balcony or patio, many outdoor bulbs can be grown in pots year after year and brought inside as they are about to flower. Acclimatize them first, gradually raising the temperature rather than bringing them straight from the cold into a warm room.

Creating a table centrepiece

Pot lilies, especially the oriental hybrids such as *Lilium longiflorum* (Easter lily) and the exotic *L.* 'Stargazer', are highly perfumed and two or three plants can scent an entire room. Sold singly in plastic pots, their presentation may be greatly improved by arranging them in a plastic-lined basket and then covering the pots with a thick mulch of moss. Make the most of this exotic display by positioning the basket on a low table in the centre of the room, where it can be appreciated fully.

1 Choose a basket that is ready-lined, or cover the bottom and sides with a sheet of plastic, fixing the edges with wire.

2 As the flower buds mature and open the stems may become quite top-heavy, so use several branches of contorted willow as supports.

RIGHT Kept cool and regularly watered, the flowers should last for several weeks. The plants are best discarded after this time.

Winter

ABOVE In winter, when cut flowers tend to be less plentiful, flowering houseplants can provide seasonal colour. Primula obconica are available in virtually every colour and suit every style of furnishings.

Indoors, winter can be far from dreary. Cyclamen will provide plenty of colour during the darkest months, as will *Rhododendron simsii* (azalea), *Euphorbia pulcherrima* (pointsettia) and the vibrantly hued *Primula obconica*.

PROTECTION AGAINST THE ELEMENTS

Frost is most plants' biggest enemy and one severe attack can wipe out an entire colony of patio plants. Frostproof planters will not crack in severe temperatures and lagging large pots safeguards both container and plant. A thick bandage of tarpaulin or an old blanket tied firmly in place with rope and covered with plastic provides a warm waterproof jacket. A downfall of snow can actually be beneficial to plants as it leaves a thick insulating crust on the soil, which again protects the roots from a subsequent frost. Snow should be gently shaken off evergreen plants as the weight of it may break the branches.

Although ground frost may not attack window boxes and balcony gardens, plants in these positions may need extra protection against freezing winds. Long periods of warmer winds, on the other hand, can dry out containers very quickly and watering may need to be as regular as

OPPOSITE Plants may have to be moved to a brighter position during the winter months. They will need a constant temperature with increased humidity in centrally heated apartments, or the leaf tips will tend to turn brown.

*O*utdoor gardens are for the most part dormant during winter while plants, trees and shrubs take a well-earned rest. Unless the weather is very dry, they need little or no attention as their well-established roots can absorb sufficient water to sustain them through an inactive period. Plants grown in containers on the balcony and patio may, however, need the occasional drench if they are protected from heavy rain or if the season proves exceptionally dry.

in summer if the window boxes are full of winter-flowering plants.

Inside the apartment, where temperatures are more easily controlled, the most common problem is overwatering. More plants are killed by too much water than too little, and overwatering is as much a form of neglect as forgetting about your plants altogether. Apart from water-loving plants such as *Cyperus alternifolius*, no plant likes to have its roots continually in water as this vital

life-support system also needs good air circulation to survive and thrive. Plants that will need frequent watering at this time of the year are winter-flowering varieties bought in bud or about to bloom from the previous year.

WINTER COLOUR

There is a wealth of brightly coloured plants that are available all through the winter. *Cyclamen persicum*, *Jasminum polyanthum*, *Rhododendron simsii* (azalea) and

Euphorbia pulcherrima (poinsettia) are some of the most popular.

Cyclamen persicum originates from the countries surrounding the Mediterranean where it grows in semi-shade in a poor alkaline soil. Not only can it stand cool conditions and the much-reduced light from a north-facing window (south-facing in the Southern hemisphere), but it can also tolerate mild frosts, making it an excellent candidate for winter window boxes. The range of colours available in

LEFT *The rich, jewel-like colours of* Saintpaulia (*African violet*) *flowers can last for weeks. Originally only available in purple, these plants now have single, double, frilled and bicoloured flowers in pinks, blues and white.*

the modern hybrids includes every shade of pink, red, white and purple and many new bi-colour combinations. And while bright vibrant colour is exciting, white cyclamen planted with white-edged *Hedera helix* (common ivy) make a very sophisticated window box. Indoors, a group of white cyclamen could be grouped with other plants which like a cool temperature in winter. *Laurus*, *Fatsia*, *Euonymus* and *Tolmiea* all prefer a low 10–13°C (50–55°F) resting period.

Cyclamen appreciate being stood in a saucer of wet pebbles so that the roots are not in contact with the water. Grouping them together also increases the level of moisture circulation around the leaves. Regular feeding will keep cyclamen in flower for the longest period, but watering must be from the base of the pot as wet tubers rot very easily, causing the entire plant to wilt. Kept cool, cyclamen can bloom for six to eight weeks, after which time they should be

discarded unless there is space to keep them. The plants need to be kept dry until the following autumn when the tubers will need fresh compost.

Rhododendron simsii (azalea) are usually bought in bloom in late autumn; plants with plenty of well-rounded, coloured buds are a better purchase than fully open flowers. Every tone of pink, red and orange in both single and double, bi- or tri-coloured flowers are being bred in small, compact, bushy plants, and, more recently, thanks to the revival of topiary, in standard trees. These wonderfully exuberant plants add a real whoosh of hot colour in winter, but their brilliance cannot tolerate the dry heat from central heating. Keep them well away from radiators, increase the humidity level by placing two or three plants together in a basket large enough to conceal a tray of wet pebbles and mist the flowers every day. All rhododendron are lime haters, so always water them with rain water or boiled and cooled water. If possible, immerse the pot or at least stand it in deep water for 30 minutes.

Less flamboyant but appropriate in any style of interior are *Erica gracilis* and *Brassica oberacea acephala* (ornamental cabbage), which offer an alternative to the bright colours of spring and summer. Both are disposable plants, but their longevity will be increased if they are kept cool

BELOW A profusion of warm winter colour is provided by seasonal flowering houseplants including: (front, left to right) miniature cyclamen, Saintpaulia (African violet); (back, left to right) azalea, cymbidium orchid, jasmine, poinsettia and cyclamen.

and away from radiators and draughts. Combine them together in a large, shallow container, using either the white-flowering *Erica* and cream and green *B. oberacea acephala* or a group of the maroon and purple varieties.

For unlimited colour choice, *Primula obconica* is a bushy primrose that grows to about 25 cm (10 in) and produces flowers all winter in blue, white, apricot and countless red, crimson and cerise varieties. This plant is known as the poison primrose because its hairy leaves contain primin, which can cause a severe allergic

ABOVE Brassica oleracea acephala (ornamental cabbage) like cool conditions and will survive quite happily outside provided they are protected from frost.

reaction in some people. This unfortunate characteristic is slowly being bred out of these pretty plants, but care is still needed. *P. obconica* should be discarded after it has flowered, but its close cousin, *P. malacoides*, may well go on to produce flowers for a second season if it is rested during the summer months and repotted into a humus-rich compost.

Specially prepared bulbs planted in late summer and early autumn will flower between mid- and late winter and include *Iris recticulata*, *Galanthus nivalis* (snowdrop), *Muscari* (grape hyacinth), hyacinths, narcissi and crocuses. If planted at intervals during the autumn, these plants will provide refreshing colour from early to mid-winter onwards.

WINTER FRAGRANCE

Many of the original species of cyclamen are scented and, although this has been bred out of the modern hybrids, there are some new miniature varieties that have a faint perfume. A winter-flowering plant that is renowned for its perfume is *Jasminum polyanthum*. Available to buy in late winter, this is often sold trained around a wire hoop in a garland shape. Unlike the garden varieties, *J. polyanthum* comes from the Far East where it vigorously climbs trees in humid and semi-shady conditions. Reproduce its habitat as closely as possible and it will flower profusely for several months. The difficulty usually lies in achieving sufficient humidity in centrally heated rooms. Daily

misting may be the only solution to prevent the buds dropping off before they mature into fragrant clusters of star-shaped flowers. One plant is enough to scent a room, and when it has finished flowering it can be discarded, unless it can be moved to a conservatory or greenhouse. This is another plant that appreciates a summer break on a warm balcony or patio.

PLANTS FOR CHRISTMAS

Winter, and in particular Christmas, is often associated with *Euphorbia pulcherrima*

ABOVE Caladium bicolor *is grown for its highly decorative leaves which may be bi- or tricoloured. It prefers a winter temperature of around 13°C (55°F) and lots of humidity.*

(poinsettia), a Mexican plant with flamboyant red bracts that resemble large, showy flowers. Modern technology has resulted in new cultivars with wonderful yellow, pink and apricot bracts, which provide a more subtle alternative to the original red or creamy-white variety. *E. pulcherrima* will remain in flower for about two months if kept warm and in

bright light, and then should be discarded as it needs a very complicated cultivation in order to flower again.

A Christmas time plant that will bloom again each year is *Zygocactus truncatus* (Christmas cactus), a succulent cactus whose ancestors came from the Orgel mountains in Brazil. Between late autumn and late winter the tips of the plant's leaves develop long, coloured buds which

ABOVE A Phalaenopsis *(moth orchid) provides a touch of luxury in winter. Teamed with a terracotta candle holder and decorated with nuts and cones, it forms a sophisticated display.*

open into truly exotic white, cerise, purple or violet flowers. In late spring move *Z. truncatus* outside into a bright position protected from direct sun and slugs, and leave it there until it is time

to bring it indoors again in the autumn. The shorter periods of daylight in autumn and winter actually stimulate the development of its flowers. This is a plant to be nurtured and treasured because the rewards are spectacular, although in the Northern hemisphere the inconsistencies in the climate and light levels may affect the flowering period from year to year.

Creating a scented basket

Plants make splendid gifts at any time of the year but particularly in winter, when a splash of vivid living colour can brighten up a cold day. With a little forward planning, you can start growing a collection of different bulbs in late autumn so that they will be just about to flower in time for Christmas. Buy bulbs from late summer onwards, or choose semi-mature plants on which the buds have started to appear and repot them in your own decorative containers.

1 Line a basket with a piece of plastic and carefully remove each bulb from its growing pot without disturbing its fragile roots too much.

2 Pack the bulbs closely together so they provide support for one another and fill the gaps, and then cover the surface with a thick mulch of moss to hold in the moisture.

ABOVE Place the basket in a bright spot, free from draughts and away from any direct heat. Keep the compost and moss moist and turn the basket occasionally so the flowers and leaves develop evenly.

Choosing plants for seasonal colour

SPRING

Abutilon

Beloperone guttata

Brunfelsia

Calceolaria

Clivia miniata

Crocus

Cyclamen

Dianthus

Exacum affine

Fuchsia

Hippeastrum

Hyacinthus

Hydrangea

Impatiens

Ipomoea purpurea

Jasminum officinale

Lantana camara

Medinilla magnifica

Narcissus

Nertera granadensis

Oxalis triangularis

Pachystachys lutea

Passiflora caerulea

Rhipsalidopsis gaertneri

Rhododendron simsii

Schizanthus retusus

Sinningia

Tulipa

Zantedeschia

SUMMER

Abutilon

Acalpha hispida

Achimenes hybrida

Begonia elatior

Bougainvillea

Bouvardia

Celosia

Citrus mitis

Clivia miniata

Dahlia

Dianthus

Exacum affine

Fuchsia

Gloriosa rothschildiana

Hibiscus rosa-sinensis

Hydrangea

Impatiens

Ipomoea purpurea

Leptospermum scoparium

Mimosa pudica

Nerium oleander

Nertera granadensis

Osteospermum

Oxalis triangularis

Pachystachys lutea

Passiflora caerulea

Pelargonium

Plumbago

Sinningia

Stephanotis floribunda

Streptocarpus

Thunbergia alata

Torenia fournieri

Zantedeschia

Begonia elatior

Rhipsalidopsis gaertneri

Sinningia

AUTUMN

Acalypha hispida
Achimenes hybrida
Allamanda cathartica
Aphelandra squarrosa
Begonia elatior
Bougainvillea
Calceolaria
Callistephus
Celosia
Citrus mitis
Cyclamen
Erica
Hibiscus
Hippeastrum
Hydrangea
Plumbago
Schizanthus retusus
Solanum
Thunbergia alata

WINTER

Acacia
Clivia miniata
Crocus
Cyclamen
Cytisus
Erica
Euphorbia pulcherrima
Hippeastrum
Hyacinthus
Jasminum officinale
Muscari
Narcissus
Primula acaulis
Rhododendron simsii
Scilla sibirica
Solanum
Tulipa
Zantedeschia
Zygocactus truncatus

Cymbidium

FLOWERING PLANTS
AVAILABLE ALL YEAR ROUND

Aechmea
Ananas comosus
Anthurium
Begonia elatior
Browallia
Calathea crocata
Campanula isophylla
Cattleya
Chrysanthemum indicum
Clerodendrum thomsoniae
Columnea
Crossandra
Cymbidium
Gardenia jasminoides

Gerbera
Guzmania
Hoya bella
Hydrangea
Kalanchoe blossfeldiana
Lilium
Miltonia
Phalaenopsis
Primula
Saintpaulia
Spathiphyllum
Stephanotis floribunda
Streptocarpus
Tillandsia
Vriesea

Achimenes hybrida

PRACTICALITIES

The basic skills of indoor gardening are easy to acquire
and the simple techniques of watering, feeding, potting
and transplanting need only common sense and a little
practical experience. As your confidence and expertise
develop, so too will your ability to grow and
propagate more demanding plants.

Equipment and Materials

*U*nlike an outdoor garden which ideally requires a potting shed or similar outhouse to contain all its vital tools and materials, the indoor-garden essentials are minimal. A small hand fork and trowel will be needed for repotting plants, and a watering can with a long, narrow spout makes watering easier — particularly when plants are in high or awkward positions. Keep separate spray bottles for dispensing water, insecticides and foliar fertilizer, marking them clearly to avoid confusion. Always make sure, too, that insecticides and fertilizers are kept out of children's reach. A pair of sharp, heavy-duty scissors or secateurs is needed for pruning, and a selection of bamboo or wooden stakes for stem supports. Houseplants are often sold with their stems attached to stakes with strips of plastic or wire. It is more attractive to replace these with green garden twine or natural coloured raffia in the home.

Unless you have a lot of storage space, it may be impractical to keep bags of potting mixture in your apartment. It is easier to buy one economical bag as and when a number of plants need repotting, and then to have one big planting session. In this way you will also save on the cost of buying new plant pots, as a small plant can be repotted into a larger pot vacated by another. Never be tempted to use garden soil for repotting houseplants as it often contains pests, fungal-disease spores and weed seeds. Choose a good multi-purpose fertilizer to promote the growth of your plants: fertilizers that are applied directly to the compost are available as slow-release pills, plant sticks, and as concentrates which must be diluted with water; foliar feeds are also diluted with water, but are sprayed on to the leaves of plants.

As a final hint, always be on the lookout for new and interesting containers. Keep a good selection of pots, as you would a collection of versatile vases, so that they are ready and waiting for any spontaneous purchases of new plants, particularly the seasonal and short-lived flowering varieties.

BELOW Shells, pebbles, glass marbles, potpourri and pine cones may all be used to line a glass planter and disguise a functional pot. Shells and pebbles can also conceal dark compost.

LEFT An essential list of gardening equipment includes: a watering can with a long spout and a fine rose attachment; a plant mister; sterile potting compost; terracotta pots and drip trays; green canes for plant supports; terracotta crocks for drainage; green twine for tying plants; secateurs and gardeners' scissors; a fork and trowel; coarse gravel and moss for water-retaining mulches.

Routine Plant Care

Often the automatic reaction to see-ing a plant in distress is to assume that lack of water is the cause, but more plants are killed by overwatering than by any other form of neglect. Only water plants when the compost has dried out but before the plant has started to be affected by lack of water – that is, before the leaves start to droop. Most plants appreciate being stood in deep water for between 30 minutes and an hour and then allowed to drain off before being returned to their original position. Some, but very few, plants actually prefer to be stood continuously in water; *Cyperus* and other semi-aquatic plants are prime examples. Standing other types of plant in water in this way will actively harm them; the soil will become waterlogged and their roots will eventually rot.

If a plant is too big to be immersed in water, water from the top using a water-ing can with a long, narrow spout to avoid splashing the leaves. *Saintpaulia* (African violet) and cyclamen should always be watered from the bottom as it is difficult to avoid getting water on their delicate leaves and stems. Bromeliads have special requirements; they need water poured into their central cup, which must never be allowed to dry out.

LEFT Watering once a week is usually sufficient for most plants, except in very hot weather when they may require a more frequent dose.

LEFT Daily misting is much appreciated by many humidity-loving plants, such as ferns, and it also reduces dust on leaves. Use tepid water and ideally mist your plants in the morning so that there is time for the leaves to dry before night fall.

LEFT _Most plants
will thrive in a
humid microclimate.
Stand their pots on
terracotta feet and
fill the drip trays
with stones surrounded
with water._

FAR LEFT _Some plants,
such as_ Cyperus, _like
their roots to be
constantly wet, and will
thrive if planted in a
tank filled with pebbles
and 5–8 cm (2–3 in)
of water. This will also
increase the humidity
around the leaves._

HUMIDITY LEVELS

With the exception of bright-sun lovers, raising the level of humidity will benefit virtually all plants, and a good degree of moisture in the air also prevents plants drying out so quickly. Covering the top of the pot with a mulch of moss or a layer of stones or shells not only looks more attractive than the sight of black soil, but it also helps to prevent excess water evaporation. Placing plants on a tray of wet pebbles, ensuring that the bases of the pots are not in contact with the water, immediately raises the level of humidity around the plants, allowing the leaves to absorb the evaporating water from the atmosphere.

Misting plants every day will certainly improve the texture of the leaves and keep them free of dust, but it will only improve the humidity for a few minutes. In summer, when windows are open and there is good air circulation, the problem is less severe; in winter, with the dry atmosphere caused by central heating, raising the level of humidity is essential. A humidifier, preferably one with an air-circulation fan, is ideal for plants and also has the benefit of creating a much healthier environment for humans.

FEEDING

Plants also need feeding to encourage healthy growth and flowering. This is usually necessary in late spring and during the summer months or when a plant is coming out of a seasonal resting period. New plants or recently repotted plants do not need feeding for at least six to eight weeks as there will be plenty of nutrients in the fresh soil. Liquid feeding is probably the easiest method as you simply give a small dose of fertilizer every time you water the plants during the growing season. Slow-release pills or sticks, however, will supply plants with nutrients for several months. Over-feeding is another classic form of neglect, as too much fertilizer, while encouraging lots of leaves, will inhibit flowering and if seriously overdone can cause the plants to die.

Repotting Plants

*E*very year or so most houseplants will need repotting, and the best season to do this is spring when the roots will have time to re-establish themselves before the resting period. Classic signs for repotting are when the soil dries out very quickly after watering, when growth is slow even with regular feeding and – the most obvious sign of all – when masses of roots are growing out through the drainage holes in the base of the pot.

Some plants, such as *Saintpaulia* (African violet), actually prefer to be kept pot-bound as this helps to promote flowering. Bromeliads are another exception and will never need repotting as the soil they are in merely provides a stable base for the plant, not a means of nourishment.

It is more economical, if possible, to repot a group of plants at the same time, as one vacated pot will invariably provide a new and bigger home for another, and so on. For the majority of plants use a multi-purpose compost when repotting.

1 ◀ *Unless the pot is brand new, wash and scrub it inside and out to eliminate any pests or diseases. Fill the base of the pot with a handful of broken crocks to ensure good drainage.*

2 ▲ *Use the existing plant pot as a mould and fill the bottom and sides of the new pot with fresh, sterile potting compost.*

Exceptions include orchids and cacti which like a specially prepared mixture, and *Rhododendron simsii* (azalea) and *Sparmannia africana* (house lime) which are both lime-hating plants and prefer an acid soil. New pots should be perfectly clean, so make sure you wash pots that have been vacated by other plants – especially those that have been standing outside – in order to prevent the possible spread of diseases or pests among your plants.

Before repotting any plant, ensure that it has good drainage by covering the drainage holes with a thick layer of

crocks – broken pieces of a clay pot or stones. You may prefer to keep large specimens in their existing pots, especially if the pot has been carefully chosen to enhance the plant. If so, you can apply the quick technique of top dressing. This involves removing approximately 5 cm (2 in) of soil from the top of the pot and replacing it with fresh compost.

RIGHT When a plant has reached its optimum size or if the pot is already quite large, you may prefer not to repot and it is possible to refresh the soil by top dressing.

3 ▲ *Leave a small gap at the top of the new pot and press the soil down gently. Carefully remove the old pot to leave a hole exactly the size of the plant.*

4 ▶ *Place the plant gently into the soil without disturbing its roots and add a thin layer of compost to the top of the pot. Water well and ideally replace the plant in its previous position.*

Simple Propagation

In late spring and summer when light levels are at their maximum and the temperature is generally warm, it is possible to multiply some of your plants by means of simple propagation. It is immensely pleasurable to grow new plants for your collection and they will also make very satisfying and personal gifts for family and friends. By far the easiest method is to take stem cuttings. *Hedera* (ivy), tradescantia, *Plectranthus* and *Sparmannia africana* (house lime) are just some of the varieties which may be propagated in this way. Take a piece of stem between 8–14 cm (3–5 in) long and make a clean cut just below a leaf. Remove most of the leaves and stand the cutting in a glass of water in a light position, making sure that no leaves are in contact with the water where they will rot. Within a week or so roots will start to appear, and when they have grown to about 2.5–4 cm (1–1½ in) long the new plant is ready to pot. You may need to change the water regularly as green slime may develop, polluting the water and preventing healthy root growth.

Some plants produce tiny plantlets either at the ends of trailing stems or on top of their leaves. These include *Chlorophytum comosum* (spider plant),

Saxifraga stolonifera (mother of thousands) and *Tolmiea menziesii* (piggyback plant). These plantlets may be planted directly into soil or you could stand them in water as previously described.

Saintpaulia (African violet), leaf begonias and many succulents are best propagated by taking leaf cuttings. Press a single leaf with about 5 cm (2 in) of stalk into a rooting medium, usually an equal mixture of peat and coarse sand. Placing the pot in a plastic bag or a propagator will increase the humidity and warmth and will speed up root development.

Monstera deliciosa (Swiss cheese plant) and many *Philodendron* varieties can become rather straggly as they grow older, and these plants can be divided into several plants by taking cuttings from stems with noticeable root nodules at their bases. Cutting the stem below the nodule and standing it in water in good light will produce roots in a couple of weeks and eventually, when potted, a new and compact plant. Use a transparent container such as a vase, large glass or jam jar because light is needed to stimulate root growth.

ABOVE *Many houseplants can be propagated very easily from stem cuttings. In late spring through to early autumn,* Plectranthus, *tradescantia,* Anthurium, Chlorophytum *(spider plant) and* Hedera Helix *(common ivy) develop roots in a week or so if placed in a well-lit window.*

TAKING LEAF CUTTINGS

1 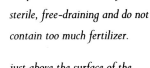 *Cut a mature leaf, with about 5 cm (2 in) of stalk attached, from the base of the* plant. Make a clean, straight cut using a razor blade or sharp knife.

2 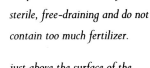 *Fill a pot with rooting medium; the specially formulated seed and cutting* composts are ideal as they are sterile, free-draining and do not contain too much fertilizer.

3 ◀ *Make a hole with a pencil at a 45° angle and insert the cutting with the back of the leaf towards the outside of the pot. The base of the leaf should be* just above the surface of the compost. Press the soil gently around the stalk. Two or three cuttings can be inserted in each pot, if wished.

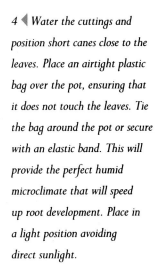

4 ◀ *Water the cuttings and position short canes close to the leaves. Place an airtight plastic bag over the pot, ensuring that it does not touch the leaves. Tie the bag around the pot or secure with an elastic band. This will provide the perfect humid microclimate that will speed up root development. Place in a light position avoiding direct sunlight.*

What Can Go Wrong

*V*ery few plants last forever and some are only really intended to live for a season, after which they are best discarded. Sometimes environmental conditions, pests, diseases or incorrect treatment can cause a plant to show signs of ill-health and eventually to die. However, if the symptoms are recog- nized early enough the problem may be solved, and the plant should make a full recovery and in time resume its former healthy appearance.

Physical Indications

Upper Leaves Turning Yellow
Usually affects lime-hating plants, such as *Rhododendron simsii* (azalea) and *Sparmannia* (house lime), and is caused by watering with hard water containing too much calcium. Use boiled or filtered water only for watering.

Brown Spots or Patches on Leaves
May be due to insect infestation, too much direct sunlight or splashing water on the leaves of plants such as *Saintpaulia* (African violet).

Leaves Curling at the Edges and Dropping
May be caused by too cool an atmosphere, overwatering or placing the plant in the way of a cold draught.

Brown Tips and Edges of Leaves
The most usual culprit is too little humidity and too much direct sun. Occasionally it may also be attributed to over- watering or overfeeding.

Wilting Leaves
Underwatering is the most likely cause. However, if the soil is waterlogged, caused by insufficient drainage or perma- nently standing the plant in water, then overwatering may be the reason. In this case the roots have rotted and are unable to transport water to the rest of the plant.

Dull Leaves
Leaves that appear lifeless and dull may simply require wip- ing with a damp cloth to remove household dust and grime. However, these signs might also indicate that the plant is receiving too much light or the presence of red spider mites.

Sudden Leaf Fall
Loss of lower leaves is not uncommon in newly purchased plants, or after repotting or when a plant has been moved from one location to another. However, drastic leaf fall is caused by a major shock to the plant's system, due to a sharp rise or fall in temperature, standing the plant in an icy draught, or underwatering.

No Flowers
Usually caused by insufficient light. If the flower buds develop but drop before reaching matur- ity this is probably due to dry air or underwatering. Flowers which develop but fade quickly may be getting too much heat, too little light and not enough water.

Variegated Leaves Turning Green
Due to insufficient light which generally results in pale, small leaves and a rather leggy grow- ing habit in plants.

Rotting Leaves and Stems
Probably due to a disease and often caused by overwatering, poor drainage and providing insufficient ventilation.

Discoloration of Clay Pots
A green slimy film on pots is a definite indication of over- watering or poor drainage. A white crust deposit on the pot is either due to using hard water or overfeeding.

Pests and Diseases

Pests and diseases generally attack indoor plants far less than they do those in the garden, but it is important to inspect your plants regularly – especially in summer when they are most prone to invasion. If infestations are discovered early enough, serious damage may be avoided by applying the correct remedy immediately. Also remember that overwatering and insufficient ventilation both encourage and allow diseases to spread. Once a pest or disease has been identified, isolate the plant if you can and check the other plants in the room even more carefully.

Mealy Bug
Small insects covered with a white fluff. These pests form colonies on the leaves and in the leaf axis. Eventually the leaves turn yellow, wilt and drop off.
Treatment Wipe off bugs with alcohol-impregnated swabs or spray the plant with malathion.

Vine Weevil
A creamy-coloured grub which lives in the soil and eats the roots of the plant. The adult dark brown beetle then goes on to chew the leaves.
Treatment Damage is usually fatal as the root system is often irreversibly damaged before the problem becomes noticeable. Discarding the plant may be the only solution but, if caught early, both leaves and compost need spraying with pesticide.

Whitefly
Tiny, moth-like flies which deposit a sticky honeydew on the undersides of the leaves. Flowering plants are most vulnerable. The honeydew, which is the insects' excreta, also encourages black mould to develop.
Treatment Spray with malathion or pyrethrum every three days. Change your remedy after a couple of weeks if infestation is still apparent, as whitefly become immune to the same formula.

Red Spider Mites
Red or pink eight-legged pests that suck the sap causing black spots and yellowed leaves. They also leave black excreta on the leaves.
Treatment Remove badly affected leaves and spray the rest of the plant with malathion or a systemic insecticide.

Aphids (Greenfly)
Brown, grey or green insects which attack the plant, sucking the sap and leaving the tell-tale sticky honeydew which causes leaves to wither.
Treatment Remove pests with cotton swabs soaked in alcohol and, as an added precaution, spray the plant with a pesticide afterwards.

Snails and Slugs
Create large, uneven holes in the leaves or, when they are particularly hungry, eat the leaves entirely.
Treatment Treat organically by sinking half an empty grapefruit filled with beer in a convenient space in the soil. Slug pellets are effective but use with care if there are children and animals around.

Powdery Mildew
A fungal disease which coats the leaves with a white powdery deposit.
Treatment Remove and destroy affected leaves and spray the remaining plants with a systemic fungicide. Improve the ventilation in the room.

Black Leg (Black Stem Rot)
Affects stem cuttings, turning the bases black, and is caused by the *Botrytis* fungus.
Treatment Remove and destroy affected cuttings. This disease is often caused by an overwet soil, so use a light, well-draining medium and dip the cuttings in a hormone rooting powder containing fungicide.

Sooty Mould (Black Mould)
A black fungus which often grows on the honeydew left by aphids and mealy bugs.
Treatment Wipe off the mould using well-diluted soapy water and eradicate the insects which produce the sticky honeydew.

Botrytis (Grey Mould)
Grey, fluffy mould which can cover the plant and is caused by growing plants in a cool and damp atmosphere with poor air circulation.
Treatment Remove affected parts and spray with systemic fungicide. Move plants to a warmer and drier location, and improve ventilation.

Advice on Buying

*I*t does not really matter where you choose to buy your plants provided you check them carefully to ensure that they are in peak condition. Reputable garden centres, nurseries and plant specialists are safe choices as they are usually run by enthusiastic experts who stock a good range of plants in controlled conditions and can offer well-informed advice to their customers. Plants sold from dark corners or kept on draughty, cold floors may be dying before you buy them. Tender, tropical plants – which is what most houseplants are – should never be bought from outside locations; the damage they will inevitably have suffered may not be apparent until after you have got them home. Houseplants should always be sold from an inside position, preferably in a well-ventilated greenhouse or conservatory. The exception is the range of varieties that benefit from a spell outdoors during summer.

Green plants should have lots of growing shoots and firm, spotless leaves. Avoid plants with brown or curling leaf edges, yellow or brown spots on the leaves or branches with wide gaps between leaves. Good retailers provide a care card with each plant describing the plant and its preferred position, watering and feeding

LEFT Good plant retailers will supply plants in plastic or paper sleeves, which protect leaves and flowers, and a purpose-made tray to hold the plants safely on the journey home.

requirements and any other important information such as if it is poisonous. Flowering plants should have lots of fat, coloured buds. Do not be tempted to buy plants with immature green buds in the belief that the flowers will last longer, as in fact the buds will probably never open at all. Plants such as *Spathiphyllum*, *Stephanotis*, *Anthurium* and all the orchid family are best bought in flower, otherwise it may be a year before they blossom, and if conditions are not ideal, you may never see them flower.

As well as inspecting for leaf damage, also check for any signs of insect infestation, or you may infect all the other plants

in your apartment. If you are in doubt about the suitability of a particular variety, ask for help and accurately describe the place a plant is intended for – an east-facing window, a shady bathroom, a centrally heated living room, for example. If the retailer does not have the plant you require, enquire whether they can source it for you. Many large specimens are not regularly stocked but should be available to order.

Finally, do take containers with you when buying plants. Seeing your choice of planter, an imaginative retailer may be able to suggest varieties you may not have considered.

S u p p l i e r s

Clifton Nursery
Clifton Villas
London W9 2PH
0171-289 6851
*Houseplants, containers including antique
flower pots*

The Garden Studio
146 Columbia Road
London E2 7RG
0171-613 2424
Old and new terracotta pots

Hare Lane Pottery
Cranborne
near Wimbourne
Dorset BH21 2QT
01725 517700
Terracotta pots

Ned Heywood
Workshop Gallery
13 Lower Church Street
Chepstow
Gwent NP6 5HJ
01291 624836
Glazed planters

Jane Hogben Ceramics
Grove House
East Common
Gerrards Cross
Bucks SL9 7AF
01753 882364
(telephone for nearest stockist)

Patio
155 Battersea Park Road
London SW8 4BU
0171-622 8262
Small to giant-size terracotta pots

Pots and Pithoi
The Barns
East Street
Turners Hill
West Sussex RH10 4QQ
01342 714793
(telephone for nearest stockist)

Woodhams
60 Ledbury Road
London W11 2AJ
0171-243 3141
*Interior design service, plants and
exclusive pots*

Marston Exotics
Brampton Lane
Madley
Herefordshire HR2 9LX
01981 251140
Insectivorous plant specialist

Fibrex Nurseries
Honeybourne Road
Pebworth
Stratford-upon-Avon
Warwickshire CV37 8XT
Fern specialist

Livelands Nurseries
119–121 London Road
Marks Tey
Colchester
Essex CO6 1EB
01206 210504
Arum lily specialist

Ceramdela Ltd
Chelsea Business Centre
334 Queenstown Road
London SW8 4NE
0171-498 0960
Ceramic pots
(telephone for nearest stockist)

Keith Butters (Plants) Ltd
Kellet Gate
Spalding
Lincs PE12 6EH
01775 768831
Major importer of house and patio plants

Hollington Nurseries
Wootten Hill
Newbury
Berks RG15 9XT
01635 253908
Herb specialist

Avant Garden
77 Ledbury Road
London W11 2AG
0171-229 4408
Glass, ceramic and wire planters
(telephone for nearest stockist)

Holly Gate Cactus Nursery
Billinghurst Road
Ashington
West Sussex RH20 3BA
01903 892930
Cactus specialist

Eaton Shell Shop
30 Neal Street
London WC2
0171-379 6254
Shells and precious stones
(mail order)

Habitat
*Ceramic and metal planters, baskets
and pots*
(40 stores nationwide, telephone
01645 334433 for nearest branch)

Ikea
*Ceramic, terracotta and metal containers
and baskets*
(5 superstores, telephone 0181-451
5566 for nearest store)

MKM Nurseries
Bulls Lane
Bell Bar
Nr Hatfield
Herts AL9 7AZ
01707 649366
Major supplier of houseplants

Chryssie Lowe
41A Allfarthing Lane
London SW18
0181-874 9422
Stencilled pots to commission

Jackson & Perkins
P.O. BOx 1028
Medford, OR 97501, USA
1 800 292 4769
(mail order)

David Kay
1 Jenni Lane
Peoria, IL, USA
1 800 535 9917
(mail order)

Smith & Hawken
117 East Strawberry Drive
Mill VAlley, CA 94941, USA
1 415 389 8300
(mail order)

The Gardener's Supply Company
128 Intervale Road
Burlington, VT 05401, USA
1 802 863 1700
(mail order)

Gardeners' Eden
P.O. Box 7307
San Francisco, CA 94120, USA
1 800 822 9600
(mail order)

Glossary of common plant names

Abutilon flowering maple

Acacia mimosa

Acalypha hispida chenille plant

Achimenes hybrida cupid's bower

Acorus gramineus sweet flag

Adiantum maidenhair fern

Aechmea fasciata urn plant, vase plant

Aglaonema commutatum Chinese evergreen

Allamandra cathartica golden trumpet

Ananas bracteatus striatus red pineapple

Ananas comosus ivory pineapple

Anthurium scherzerianum flamingo flower

Aphelandra squarrosa zebra plant, saffron spike

Arabis caucasica a rock plant

Araucaria heterophylla Norfolk Island pine

Argyranthemum frutescens marguerite

Asparagus asparagus fern

Aspidistra elatior cast-iron plant

Asplenium nidus bird's-nest fern

Aubretia deltoidea rock cress

Bambusa vulgaris common bamboo

Beaucarnea recurvata elephant's foot, pony tail

Begonia boweri eyelash begonia

Begonia elatior begonia

Begonia rex rex begonia

Beloperone guttata shrimp plant

Bougainvillea glabra paper flower

Bouvardia domestica jasmine plant

Bouvardia ternifolia scarlet trompetilla

Brassica oleracea acephala ornamental cabbage

Browallia bush violet

Brunfelsia yesterday, today and tomorrow

Caladium hortulanum angel's wings

Calathea crocata peacock plant

Calathea makoyana peacock plant

Calathea zebrina zebra plant

Calceolaria herbeohybrida slipper flower, pocket-book plant

Calendula pot marigold

Callisia striped inch plant

Callistephus Chinese aster

Camellia camellia

Campanula bellflower

Campanula isophylla Italian bellflower, star of Bethlehem

Capsicum annuum ornamental chilli pepper

Capsicum grossum sweet pepper

Caryota mitis Burmese fishtail palm

Catharanthus roseus Madagascar periwinkle

Cattleya corsage orchid

Celosia cockscomb

Cereus peruvianus column cactus

Chamaedorea elegans parlour palm

Chamaerops humilis fan palm

Chlorophytum comosum spider plant

Chrysalidocarpus lutescens areca palm, yellow palm

Chrysanthemum morifolium pot chrysanthemum

Citrus mitis calamondin orange

Clerodendrum thomsoniae glory bower

Clivia miniata kaffir lily

Cocos nucifera coconut palm

Cocos weddeliana dwarf coconut palm

Codiaeum croton

Colchicum autumnale autumn crocus

Coleus blumei flame nettle

Columnea gloriosa goldfish plant

Convallaria majalis lily-of-the-valley

Cordyline fruticosa good-luck plant

Crassula argentea jade plant

Crocus crocus

Crossandra firecracker flower

Cucumis sativus cucumber

Cupressus macrocarpa a conifer

Cycas revoluta sago palm

Cyclamen persicum cyclamen

Cymbidium cymbidium orchid

Cyperus alternifolius umbrella plant

Cyperus papyrus papyrus

Cytisus canariensis Canary Island broom, genista

Dahlia dahlia

Datura candida angel's trumpet

Davallia rabbit's-foot fern

Dianthus carnation, pink

Dieffenbachia dumb cane

Dionaea muscipula Venus fly trap

Dizygotheca elegantissima false aralia

Dracaena marginata Madagascar dragon tree

Echeveria setosa Mexican firecracker

Epiphyllum orchid cactus

Erica carnea Alpine heath

Erica gracilis cape heath

Euonymus spindle tree

Euphorbia milii crown of thorns

Euphorbia pulcherrima poinsettia

Eustoma grandiflorum prairie gentian

Exacum affine Persian violet

Fatshedera lizei ivy tree

Fatsia japonica Japanese aralia, castor-oil plant

Ficus benghalensis banyan tree, Bengal fig

Ficus benjamina weeping fig

Ficus elastica rubber plant

Ficus longifolia ornamental fig

Ficus lyrata fiddle-leaf fig

Ficus pumila creeping fig

Fittonia argyroneura silver-net leaf, nerve plant

Fittonia argyroneura nana snakeskin plant

Fittonia verschaffelti painted-net leaf, mosaic plant

Fortunella margarita kumquat

Fragaria vesca sempervirens strawberry

Freesia freesia

Fuchsia fuchsia

Galanthus nivalis snowdrop

Gardenia jasminoides Cape jasmine, common gardenia

Gerbera jamesonii Barbeton daisy, African daisy

Gloriosa rothschildiana glory lily
Guzmania lingulata major scarlet star
Gymnocalycium a cactus

Hedera canariensis Canary Island ivy
Hedera helix common ivy
Helianthus annus sunflower
Hibiscus esculentus okra
Hibiscus rosa-sinensis Chinese hibiscus
Hippeastrum amaryllis
Howea forsteriana kentia palm
Hoya bella miniature wax plant
Hyacinthus hyacinth
Hydrangea macrophylla hydrangea
Hypoestes sanguinolenta polka-dot plant, freckle face

Impatiens hawkeri busy Lizzie, patient Lucy
Ipomoea morning glory
Iris recticulata iris

Jasminum officinale common jasmine, jessamine
Jasminum polyanthum pink jasmine

Kalanchoe blossfeldiana flaming Katy
Kalanchoe manginii Madagascar wax-bells

Lantana camara yellow sage
Lathyrus odoratus sweet pea
Laurus bay tree
Lilium auratum golden-rayed lily
Lilium longiflorum Easter lily
Lilium regale regal lily
Lilium speciosum Japanese lily
Lisianthus russelianus prairie gentian
Lobelia lobelia
Lonicera japonica Japanese honeysuckle
Lycopersicon esclentum tomato
Lysimachia nummularia creeping Jenny (moneywort)

Mammillaria a cactus
Maranta leuconeura kerchoveana prayer plant
Microlepia strigosa a fern
Miltonia pansy orchid
Mimosa pudica humble plant, sensitive plant
Monstera deliciosa Swiss cheese plant, split-leaf philodendron
Musa banana plant
Muscari armeniacum grape hyacinth
Myosotis forget-me-not

Narcissus narcissus
Nemesia nemesia
Nepenthes pitcher plant
Nephrolepis exaltata sword fern
Nerium oleander oleander
Nertera granadensis bead plant
Nicotiana affinis tobacco plant

Osteospermum osteospermum
Oxalis wood sorrel

Pachystachys lutea lollipop plant
Passiflora caerulea passion flower
Pelargonium geranium
Pelargonium peltatum ivy-leaf geranium
Pellaea rotundifolia button fern
Peperomia caperata emerald ripple
Peperomia glabella peperomia
Phalaenopsis moth orchid
Philodendron scandens sweetheart plant
Phoenix canariensis Canary Island date-palm
Phyllostachys aureas fishpole bamboo, golden bamboo

Pilea pilea
Plectranthus australis Swedish ivy
Plumbago auriculata Cape leadwort
Pogonatheram paniceum house bamboo
Primula acaulis primrose
Primula malacoides fairy primrose
Primula obconica poison primrose
Pteris cretica ribbon fern, table fern
Pteris ensiformis 'Victoriae' silver-lace fern

Radermachera China doll
Rebutia a cactus
Rhipsalidopsis gaertneri Easter cactus
Rhododendron simsii azalea
Rhoicissus capensis Cape grape
Rhoicissus rhomboidea grape ivy
Rosa chinensis minima miniature rose

Saintpaulia African violet
Sansevieria trifasciata mother-in-law's tongue, snake plant
Saponaria soapwort
Saxifraga stolonifera mother of thousands
Schefflera actinophylla umbrella tree
Schizanthus retusus butterfly flower
Scilla sibirica Siberian squill
Scindapsus aureus devil's ivy
Scindapsus pictus silver vine
Sedum stonecrop
Selaginella creeping moss
Senecio cruentus cineraria
Sinningia gloxinia
Solanum melongena ovigerum aubergine, egg plant
Solanum pseudocapsicum Jerusalem cherry
Soleirolia soleirolii baby's tears, mind your own business
Sparmannia africana house lime, African hemp

Spathiphyllum wallisii peace lily
Stephanotis floribunda wax flower, Madagascar jasmine
Strelitzia bird-of-paradise flower
Streptocarpus hybridus Cape primrose
Syngonium podophyllum goose-foot plant, arrowhead vine, nepththytis

Tetrastigma voinierianum chestnut vine
Thunbergia alata black-eyed Susan
Thymus thyme
Tillandsia lindenii blue-flowered torch
Tolmiea menziesii piggyback plant, pick-a-back plant, youth on age
Torenia fournieri wishbone flower
Tradescantia inch plant, wandering Jew
Tropaeolum majus nasturtium
Tulipa tulip

Viola wittrockiana pansy
Vriesea splendens flaming sword

Washingtonia robusta Washington palm

Yucca elephantipes spineless yucca

Zantedeschia aethiopica arum lily, calla lily
Zebrina pendula silvery inch plant
Zinnia elegans zinnia
Zygocactus truncatus Christmas cactus

Index

$\mathcal{I}$ N D E X

PICTURE CREDITS
All specially commissioned photography by Michelle Garrett; additional location photography on pages 9, 14 l, 17, 21, 46, 67 bl br, 111 and 117 by John Freeman.

The publishers would like to thank the following for permission to reproduce copyright images in this book:
Anness Publishing – pages 26, 34, 35, 42, 43, 48, 49 l r, 74 b, 75, 92 b, 93, 97, 100, 104, 120 r, 122, 124 bl br, 125; **Linda Burgess/The Flowers & Plants Association** – pages 47, 106 b, 120 l; **Camera Press** – pages 10, 13, 16, 19, 25, 28 t, 29, 31, 39 t b, 59, 61, 67 t, 73 r, 79, 81 b, 83, 85 l r, 87, 88, 89, 103, 107; **Robert Harding Picture Library** – page 14 r (Jan Baldwin); **House & Interiors** – page 82 l; **Smallbone of Devizes** – page 71; and **Elizabeth Whiting and Associates** – pages 28 b (Karl Dietrich Buhler), 32, 40 l (Tom Leighton), 77 (Tom Leighton), 82 r (Jay Patrick), 99 (Di Lewis).